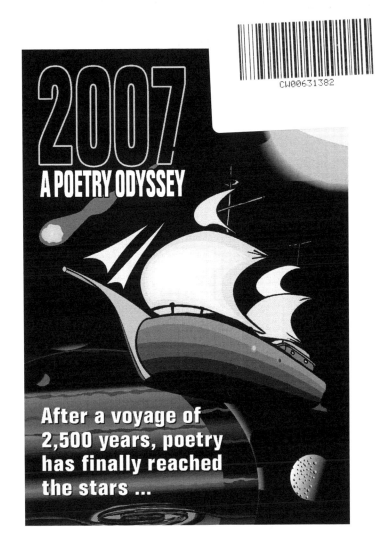

2007
A POETRY ODYSSEY

After a voyage of 2,500 years, poetry has finally reached the stars ...

Northern Verses
Edited by Angela Fairbrace

First published in Great Britain in 2007 by:
Young Writers
Remus House
Coltsfoot Drive
Peterborough
PE2 9JX
Telephone: 01733 890066
Website: www.youngwriters.co.uk

SB ISBN 978-1 84602 815 1

Foreword

This year, the Young Writers' *2007: A Poetry Odyssey* competition proudly presents a showcase of the best poetic talent selected from thousands of up-and-coming writers nationwide.

Young Writers was established in 1991 to promote the reading and writing of poetry within schools and to the young of today. Our books nurture and inspire confidence in the ability of young writers and provide a snapshot of poems written in schools and at home by budding poets of the future.

The thought, effort, imagination and hard work put into each poem impressed us all and the task of selecting poems was a difficult but nevertheless enjoyable experience.

We hope you are as pleased as we are with the final selection and that you and your family continue to be entertained with *2007: A Poetry Odyssey Northern Verses* for many years to come.

Contents

St Ambrose Barlow RC High School, Swinton

The Poems

When In The Classroom

When in the classroom
The teacher in the staffroom
I close my eyes
All the nastiness and lies
Just . . . disappear
All calm, no fear

I'm taken to a tropical land
The touch of the golden sand
Lifts me into the glistening sky
It's filled with peace and love, which makes me fly
I swim with the dolphins through the salty sea
Where up above the birds of fantasy
Fly over the wood of enchantment

I sit on the blissful beach
Listening to the wind and sea battling with each other
Watching the cygnets follow their mother
Fairies swirling and twirling around my head
Using my hair as a relaxing bed

'Wake up girl, did you hear what I said?'
Oh how I wish it wasn't all in my head . . .

Emily Nielsen (10)

Something Was There

It started on a Friday night,
Playing in the park.
I couldn't find my way home,
I was lost in the dark.

I ran across the foggy road,
It was the crematorium.
I could tell there were ghosts following me,
Suddenly I heard my mum.

I tried to run out of the graveyard,
Following her voice.
I had to go through the haunted house,
I didn't have a choice.

There were creepy-crawlies and bats
And slithery snakes too.
I stepped on a spider,
Then fell in rat poo.

There was a monster in this house,
I could feel it in the air.
Then I could smell the toxicness of the monster,
It was standing right there.

I ran for my life,
Bat flying.
I heard my mum
And started crying.

Soon I was at my house,
I ran straight upstairs.
I got under the bedclothes,
Something was there.

Amy Hyde (11)
Caldew School, Carlisle

Reaper

Even in deep, dark December
I still can't help but remember
The night the Grim Reaper killed

It was the 31st of October
In my bed I moved and rolled over
The night the Grim Reaper killed

I went downstairs for a glass of milk
When over the fridge was a cocoon of silk
On the night the Grim Reaper killed

I turned around and there he was
A myth (at least I thought it was)
On the night the Grim Reaper killed

He pulled out his staff of pain
And at that point came down the rain
I was the one the Grim Reaper killed.

Jake Reed (11)
Caldew School, Carlisle

Haunted House

It was a dark night in December,
A night I will always remember.
The only light I could see was the moon shining above me.
The ghosts and ghouls they did fly above the house
that stood way up high,
As I walked up the slippery path a bolt of lightning whizzed past.
The big oak door creaked and groaned as I trembled and shook,
But I just knew I had to take a look.
As I knocked a voice from behind said,
'Come on in, come on inside.'
As the door flung open I wanted to hide.
A witch went past on a broom just when I entered the room,
Cobwebs and spiders all over the stairs,
As I got closer I could feel their glares,
This house was too creepy, I wanted to get out,
There was no normal person anywhere about.
I was going to run, run very fast, it was just no fun it's not a blast!
As I opened the door and stepped outside I just had to run
And I never looked behind.

Kathryn Routledge (11)
Caldew School, Carlisle

Racehorse

Racehorse prepares to glide through the sky,
Canter, gallop, jump and fly.

Rain, sleet, snow and wind
As wild as cats fighting through the power,
As cold and heavy as Mount Everest.

The roses are trampled
And the leaves are turned to mud,
The hedges go rotten,
After the flood of horses aiming for gold.

Leigh Anne Stubbs (12)
Caldew School, Carlisle

Pony In The Graveyard

A small graveyard
Behind an old fallen church
In the shadows of the night.

A cold winter night
Wind is bitter through the oak tree
Standing in the graveyard.

Lying down under the oak tree
Keeping herself warm
From the cold winter weather.

The pony's coat is snowy white
She's cold and bored
With no company to warm her up.

She falls asleep
The wind blows
Her mane blows around in the wind.

The old church groans and creaks
A small shadow appears
From behind a bush.

It appears in the moonlight
A furry little creature
Not bigger than a fox.

There the pony lies
Until the dawn breaks
The next morning . . .

Roxanne Carswell (13)
Caldew School, Carlisle

The Great Golden Eagle

On an autumn hot day,
In the countryside,
An eagle flies on its way.

When the strong sun shines in the sky,
All the animals hide,
But the eagle doesn't hide away.

The eagle makes a deep scream,
It scares every single bird,
He gets hungry.

He is flying over the field,
He is looking for food,
He is feeling hot.

He is running out of patience,
Making a loud screaming noise,
Looking for food and water.

He looks, he sees,
Another bird's nest.

He goes down to the ground,
He thinks then he picks up
A stone.

He flies over the nest,
Then he comes back
And throws the stones at the eggs.

Finally the eggs are broken
And he
Finally gets his food.

Martin Lakov
Caldew School, Carlisle

Dog

On a cold, windy night
The electric goes out
People are waiting quietly

Wind blows
The door creaks open
Hundreds of figures staring at me

I run in the room barking
You can hear the pitter-patter of my feet
I am nervous of what they might do

I run around the room
My tail wagging
So excited

I want to explore
The land looks good from the inside
Then I can do what I want to do

My big, bold eyes
Are like black holes
As big as marbles

The lights go on
People are glad to see me
I go on a dog walk.

Sophie Park (12)
Caldew School, Carlisle

Great White Shark

In the middle of the Atlantic Ocean
At lunch
The great white is looking for dinner

The sneaky, scary animal
Searching for his delicious tasty
Dinner of raw seal

He makes no sound as he hunts
For the noisy seal which he plans
To eat the raw meat which he rips off the body

He moves under the water surface moving
Faster than a speedboat
And glides in the water

He can smell a lovely seal
That is injured
He can smell blood and the fear

His tail goes faster
His eyes focused
On the seal
That's moving slow

As he goes under the water
He strikes up
And eats it alive.

Kyle Moran (12)
Caldew School, Carlisle

My Dog

In the morning of summer
The sun is shining
Through the windowpane

There was a special dog called Tia
She was abandoned and unloved
Until we came along.

Now she has a loving home
And she is well looked after
Fed and groomed.

She can run as fast as a bullet
And jump as high as the moon
And likes to play with my other dog.

She has lots of different expressions
From the sad 'no one wants me'
To the 'let's go for a walk'.

She's quite a lazy dog
And sleeps all day
And she plays when she wants.

But strangest of all
She's not like any other dog
Because she never
Barks!

Sean Willis (12)
Caldew School, Carlisle

Tiger Poem

The cold, dark jungle
Anything could attack
Only the king of the jungle is safe

Prey hides trembling in trees
Predator waits for its chance
To catch and grab its prey

Jumps out viciously
With the tiger's speed
The tiger grabs and kills its prey

It's attacking, scaring
Sharp and fast
It likes to kill

Because tigers are strong
Tough and rough
Especially with their teeth

Teeth are big
Sharp as razor blades
Waiting to kill their prey

The tiger joins his family
Mouth starts to dribble
They just can't wait.

Nathan Davidson (12)
Caldew School, Carlisle

Lizard

In the rainforest
The scorching sun is rising
Creatures are talking

The undergrowth is moist and moving
Trees and plants settled everywhere
And nature shows its beauty

One of the rainforest's creatures is
A lizard searching for a feast
Using stealth so it is not seen

Looking for a meal
But the prey is hiding
The lizard soon rests

The lizard is lying in the sun's heat
With patches of shade covering it
One of the shadows moves

The lizard is now the prey
It hides under some leaves
From the predator of the skies

It looks to see if it is safe
When in swoops an eagle
To claim its prey

The lizard launches out of its path
And lands next to a meal
And *snap* it has hunted.

Sam Strong (13)
Caldew School, Carlisle

Penguins

As the sun rises
The autumn breeze howling through the Arctic
Leaving piles of snow

Snow falling on the smooth pool of frozen ice
Splashes of water freeze in mid-air
Icicles hanging from the cave entrances

Thousands of black dots gathering at the water's edge
Diving into the icy cold water
Darting after the fish for something to eat

All day and night
Wearing black and white
And pale beak makes it hard to seek.

Rebecca Harris (12)
Caldew School, Carlisle

Bobbie

In the summertime,
Sitting on the pillow,
Watching as the days go by.

In the clammy hot weather,
Her bone is buried under a feather,
She pants with tiredness.

Waiting on the stairs,
Silent . . . ready to pounce,
Ready to steal your socks.

She runs down the stairs pitter-patter, pitter-patter,
And into the garden,
She drops the sock and digs a hole.

Getting faster as her paws hit the ground,
She growls trying to dig a hole,
The hole is finally dug, she sighs.

Dropping the sock into the hole, hooray!
She is tired now, plodding back into the house,
Sighs, jumps on the pillow.

Gazing into the window her eyes are getting droopy,
Slowly, slowly, slowly she falls asleep,
Phew, she's asleep.

Stroke, stroke, pat, pat, Bobbie is calm,
She hears a noise, *bark, bark,*
She is calm again, *snorrr!*

Rebecca Firth (12)
Caldew School, Carlisle

Hallowe'en Poem

Once upon a chilly midnight,
Three children were about to get a dreadful fright.
Daring each other to open the door,
They were going to witness something scary and more.
The door creaked open wide,
A spider came scuttling from inside.
With a shock they fell in a pile of mud,
Zombies came from the ground searching for blood.
'Oh no, we're going to die,' one of them said,
Another wished he were in bed,
But the first was right, they were now all dead.

Joshua Hodkinson (11)
Caldew School, Carlisle

Homework

I go to school every day
And then they give me homework
School is for working, not home I thought
And then they give me homework
More and more it all piles up
And then they give me homework
Who made up this mad idea?
And then they give me homework
I get enough work at school
And then they give me homework
From science to French and maths to IT
And then they give me homework
It's so annoying, this mean invention
And then they give me homework
It's work that you do at home
And then they give me homework
What am I going to say next?
You guessed it
And then they give me
Homework!

Helen Brown (11)
Caldew School, Carlisle

One Gloomy Night

Once upon a cold black night
It was Hallowe'en when ghosts and ghouls come out
As I walked through the misty field
I heard the sound of howling
That went on all through the night
As I ran down the path the lights flickered
Then the wind moaned like zombies
I saw a house all spooky
And filled with dark thoughts
The cold black breeze
Ran down my spine
I walked into the house scared and frightened
I looked out the window
The bright blue moon pouring out of the clouds
I tiptoed up the stairs
A black cat ran across the creaky floorboards
With glittering blue eyes and sharp gliding claws
Down the stairs, through the door I ran
Then I woke up and saw that it was all a dream.

Emmy Gill (11)
Caldew School, Carlisle

Hallowe'en

As I walked through the blood
On a cold windy night,
I thought it was mud
And just a cold normal night.

I got a fright
When I heard a scream,
I thought it just might
Be someone falling off a beam.

I ran away
And there was a light,
I was told to obey
By something that was white.

Suddenly something small
Began to talk,
It was shaped as a ball
And started to walk.

I ran home
About to scream,
I sat still on my own
And I woke up, it was just a dream.

Sophie Kennett (11)
Caldew School, Carlisle

Hallowe'en

On the 31st October
I got a midnight fright,
I was walking through the church
When a bird perched itself on the light,
That light was shattered.
I'm sure I heard something behind,
The moon was shining on me with a dark curse light.

Black cats, scary bats, watched me as I went.
Once I got to the gate I looked round
And the black cats and scary bats were still watching.
I turned back round and saw the scary, headless monster
And that was the end of me.

Connie Betts (11)
Caldew School, Carlisle

Elephant

On a hot, grassy savannah day,
Everyone at the water hole,
Lions near their side.

A hot, hot day,
Buffalos surrounded the water hole,
Lions getting closer.

A bright, hot, dangerous day,
Trumpet of the elephant, sound of the savannah,
The lion still gets closer.

A yellow grassy day,
Skin like sandpaper,
The elephant lies in the sun.

A hot, rainless day,
Elephants tired out,
Lions eating their prey.

A hot, bright day,
Trunks waving uncontrollably,
Water hole nearly dry.

A boiling savannah day,
The elephant gets up for a drink,
But the hole is dry.

A wet rainy day,
Hole is full of mud,
There is the elephant rolling in the muck.

Ryan Stobart (12)
Caldew School, Carlisle

Black Leopard

In the deep, deep jungle
it snows
all winter long

In the morning
the snow has laid
and the jungle is great and white

Frosty and cold
everything seems dead
and cold

I am so hungry
all the herds have moved on
my black spotted skin is so cold

I am searching for some food

Then I spot my prey
a lovely ox
all alone

I duck
I crawl
I wait

The ox looks so tasty, grazing

I run
I pounce
the ox crashes to the ground

My kill is so tasty, its warm blood drips into my mouth
I am so happy, I see some more black leopards
and they come and join my blood feast.

Hanna-Leigh Hamilton (12)
Caldew School, Carlisle

Midnight Is A Minute Away

Midnight is a minute away
It's chucking it down, flooding and flooding
I feel the floor tiles are lifting.

You can't imagine the frostbite I have
All you can hear is the vent flapping
I'm being frightened to death.

My dog walks in as he gives me a glare
Then he takes the sharpest bark
As he wants my attention.

He keeps on taking small steps
Going round the room again and again
I am thinking, *what is he doing?*

I feel that my friendly dog has gone
Maybe he is scared of the weather
Like I am now.

Why is he looking at me like a tiger ready to pounce
I get out of bed to stroke him
He just runs away.

It is as if he has turned vicious
Now he is starting to growl and grunt
He starts to run as if gravity has pulled him.

Somehow my dog escapes
Why? What forced him?
Is this the end or is it a sign?

Stephanie Maxey (12)
Caldew School, Carlisle

Nightmare

This story is set in a graveyard not far from here
And as I was walking through I saw a deer.
It was in the mist, so I walked forward a little
And fell in a grave with bones, black and brittle.

As I climbed out, the deer had gone,
Instead there was a figure, singing a song.
At least I thought it was a song, but in fact it was a spell
And suddenly from nowhere, came spirits from Hell.

And from the church tower came the sound of a bell,
Heralding in the witching hour.
The spirits began to change their form,
Because the sky began to brew a storm.

The figure which rose the spirits to Earth
Turned around and there I found,
A hooded zombie with a wart-covered, flaky skinned green face,
But in seconds, it had disappeared without a trace.

I stumbled into the wood, next to the graveyard and saw
A mangled body on the floor.
It jumped up and came forth
With eyes shining like a blazing torch.

I ran as fast as I could,
The creature was howling like the wind through the trees.
I ran into the church and fell on my knees
And pleaded with God, 'Please help me, please.'

James Metcalfe (12)
Caldew School, Carlisle

Rapunzel

A little princess, vain as owt,
Would brush her hair 'til it fell out.
'Oh dear, oh my!' she then exclaimed,
'I have no hair, it is a pain.
I'll never get a prince to climb
My lovely tresses given time.'
Whilst looking through 'More' magazine
She saw the answer to her dreams.
Victoria Beckham looking glam,
With hair extensions taken from
Some poor and lowly Russian girl,
Whose head was shaved and left no curls.
Ah ha, the little princess thought,
I've loads of cash and they're all broke,
I'll shave a couple thousand heads
And have the best hair in the West.

And so she did, the wig was made,
Her hair was so long that the braid
Could wrap around her mighty tower
And gave the princess loads of power.
Her suitors came from far and wide
To view her beauty and her pride.
'Enough of this, you all are boring,
Marry you and I'll be snoring.
Enough of blokes, I'm going travelling,'
Her hair then began to start unravelling.
Whilst on a cruise she lost the wig,
Clean overboard she did a jig.
'Cause short hair's lighter and more funky,
She met a man, boy he was *hunky!*

Jessica Dobson (13)
Caldew School, Carlisle

Hallowe'en

H aunted houses stood in a row, swaying to and fro.

A witch rode by on her broom while Dracula came out of his room.

L ots of pumpkins looked very scary, so people were very weary.

L ittle bats flew everywhere, what a scare!

O wls sat in the trees, when there came a cold breeze.

W erewolves sat howling at the moon, midnight would come soon.

E verywhere was dark but then a light spark.

E vening was nearly over, then striked a cobra.

N othing was there, what a great scare!

Sarah Wilson (11)
Caldew School, Carlisle

Cloud Of Sorrow

In the happy land of Shanshanrantanwoh
All was quiet and safe
But lying above was a secret.

Watching from its darkest cloud
It scoured the land below
Waiting for his prey.

Mutants thought of this creature
Of evil breath of fire
Heart as black as coal.

A day everyone was gone
All sorrow from the cloud had spread
They believed no more.

Monster was weak
So weak he fell
To the ground.

Bang, crash, he hit the ground
The mutants came back and found
Him on the ground.

They were wrong about the beast
So beautiful of red, orange even gold
With wings so white.

With the death the mutants died
When the last leaf of life was withering
So did they.

Luke Shepherd (12)
Caldew School, Carlisle

My Button

Thinking and focused, I stare at the sky,
Just alone and wondering, I long to know why,
Why am I put here, what do I do?
The purpose of being, the meaning to you.

What can I do and where can I go?
What will I see if I go with the flow?
Pick me up and look at me,
Clean me up, then set me free.

Through pockets I've travelled of kings and men,
Through farmyards of plenty, goats, cows and hen,
I've met many people in the places I go,
Through wind and rain, through sand and snow.

I have now found my purpose, my meaning to be,
To just be a button and a button to be,
The best thing to do for you, them and me,
To be what you are, not to want what you see.

Jonathan Bellamy (14)
Egglescliffe School, Eaglescliffe

My Button!

My button is from a soldier who stood up tall and proud,
My button is from a soldier who could reach up to every cloud.
My button is from a judge with a white curly wig,
My button is from a judge who liked to do a jig.
My button is from a coachman who wore a frilly hat,
My button is from a coachman who was afraid of cats.
My button is a treasure, silvery and bold,
My button is a treasure to the young or old.

Amy Jones (11)
Egglescliffe School, Eaglescliffe

Ellie The Little Girl And Her Button

(To the tune of 'Ellie the Elephant')

Ellie the little girl
Packed her case
And waved goodbye to her mummy
Off she went with a plodity, plodity, plod, plod
She lost her elephant button
Far, far away
She cried and wept, sobbed, blubbed
For days and days and days
Then she found her button
And waved goodbye to far away.

Emily Popple (13)
Egglescliffe School, Eaglescliffe

MC Ethel

MC Ethel on the m-i-c
Rockin' up the bingo hall with Mar-jor-ie
Got a full house and shouted with glee
Cos it's my lucky number . . . twenty-three!
I then jumped up and my button just popped
It hit some geezer and my heart just stopped!
Can I have my button back?

Mrs Jackson's Tutor Group (14/15)
Egglescliffe School, Eaglescliffe

Button Poem

I came across a button one day,
Deep in a blue-cushioned box it lay,
It was tarnished and dull
And still had attached some fibres of wool.

The look of sadness in my grandmother's eyes,
As she told me of the tears she had cried,
For her long-lost love that had died.

The button on his tunic had been shiny and bright,
As he'd set off to go to war to fight,
The writing on the button was black and old,
It kept so many stories untold.

She said it was all she had to remember him by,
The brave young soldier that had to die,
As she put the button back with a mournful sigh.

Emma Relton (14)
Egglescliffe School, Eaglescliffe

Tiger Tooth

T he tiger's weapon to tear,
I see its orange and black hair,
G lory in the rainforest leaves,
E xcellent agility, as it sprints through the trees,
R oaring so loud the whole rainforest glares.

T all and fierce,
O ther animals' skin gets pierced,
O verall it's a killing machine,
T he tiger is striking and lean,
H ighest predator it is so fierce.

Liam Hill (12)
Egglescliffe School, Eaglescliffe

My Lost Button

M edium sized button
Y ellow flowers

L ost on Saturday
O ne small owner
S earching and searching
T wo holes

B eautiful button
U nusual button
T hick button
T o hold things together
O ptimists' button
N ever to be found.

Briony Wilson (12)
Egglescliffe School, Eaglescliffe

Ann Sutton's Button

There once was a girl called Ann Sutton,
Who had the most beautiful button.
It fell down the drain,
When it started to rain,
That unfortunate button of Ann Sutton.

Purple with pink flowers was that button,
That used to belong to Ann Sutton.
It would be hard to replace,
Though she searched time and space,
That unfortunate buttonless Ann Sutton.

How to fasten a coat with no button?
Was the question that faced poor Ann Sutton.
Should she use a pink pin,
Or put the coat in the bin?
That unfortunate coatless Ann Sutton.

Elizabeth Devereux (13)
Egglescliffe School, Eaglescliffe

What Really Happened
To Little Red Riding Hood

Little Red, walking through the wood,
On her way to Grandmother Hood.
Was stopped by a wolf, mouth open wide,
Whom now Miss Riding lays inside.
Granny took a stroll through the wood,
And lying there in the mud,
Something which showed Riding was dead,
A single button, bright red.

Abigail Sykes (12)
Egglescliffe School, Eaglescliffe

Teddy Bear Button/The Best Dressed Bear Contest

(A sonnet)

Oh, little yellow teddy bear (plastic),
When was it now that Baby Ben lost you?
Whose quaint gurgling was quite fantastic?
His jacket was missing a button (true),
A garment of sheer delight: incomplete.
With no teddy bear to finish it off.
Compared to my girl's clothes, it can't compete.
Three buttons down one side. (Three?) Not enough.
Baby Ben didn't realise, no. But,
His mother did, and when she found it out,
My salary (how could she do it?) Cut.
All I wanted was him, once, not perfect.
To see the expression on your smug face.
When, seeing your boy's clothes with this defect,
Would put you in your rightful place.

Connie Vaughan (13)
Egglescliffe School, Eaglescliffe

Cerberus, The Three-Headed Dog

Guardian of Hell,
In battle he fell,
To lose his canine tooth
Then Hades saw,
He fell to the floor
To be stabbed by Hercules' sword!

Cerberus rose,
Hercules froze,
Then jumped on the monster's back,
He pulled out his sword,
Cerberus 'pawsed'
Then fell to the floor in pain,
He picked up the tooth
And threw it away . . .

And till this day
There it lay
To be found by 7GD.

Matty Bone (11) & Chris Jackman (12)
Egglescliffe School, Eaglescliffe

Evolution

When life was first formed it was small, insignificant
Amoebas the initial creation
They slowly developed into animals, like apes
Devoid of an education.

Some Homo sapiens came into being,
From flint they made weapons and tools.
They hunted, they fished and they battled with ease
But their language portrayed them as fools.

Then slowly, over time, mankind was moulded
Into the form it takes today
Humans are now the main influence on Earth
Which leads us on to say:

'The strongest, fastest and smartest survive
And so we produce the solution
They key to our growth, variation and life
Is a process we call evolution.'

Sarah Dransfield (14)
Fairfield High School for Girls, Droylsden

Hello, Good Morning

Hello, good morning, how do you do?
I admit, I've never met someone like you,
How does it feel to be swimming out there?
A fun-loving being, with free time to spare.

Hello, good morning, are you feeling well?
I don't think I've met you, I simply can't tell.
I've been here so long, it feels like forever,
I doubt if I've seen you, I swear, I have never.

Hello, good morning, have you lost your way?
Although you're the first person I've seen today.
I'm sure I'd remember if I'd seen your face,
But not many come here, not in this place.

Hello, good morning, are you from round here?
I think I'd remember if I'd seen you near.
You look familiar, are we related?
I understand you can't be associated.

Hello, good morning, my time has run out,
We could meet again, but highly I doubt.
It's best if I go back to what I had started,
Run along, go ahead, it's time that we parted.

Amy Reid (15)
Fairfield High School for Girls, Droylsden

I Walk, I Buzz, I Fly

I'm the Tarantula Hawk Wasp
The baddest of the lot
I'll kill that great big spider
And use it as a cot.

I walk, I buzz, I fly
I'm cunning and I'm sly
First I'll kill that spider then I'll lay my eggs inside her
Humans say I'm the humble bumblebee
A great big stripy fly
But if they catch me in action
I'm sure to make them cry.

I walk, I buzz, I fly
I'm cunning and I'm sly
First I'll kill that great big spider
And then I'll lay my eggs inside her.

Jade Reid (14)
Fairfield High School for Girls, Droylsden

How Small?

Quiet, dignified, unassuming
The Marie Curie of the universe
The only one to dream
And the only one to have dreamt
The ears above a cricket's knees
And a moving island inching slowly
86,400 seconds in a day
The first and last 24 hours of a dragonfly's life
A road trip to the nearest star
Only 48 million years away
A black widow spider
Eating her mate
A flutterby
A jumping flea
130 times bigger than its own height
An alarmed horned toad
Squirting blood from his eyes
A bolt of lightning
Hotter than the sun's surface
A duck's quack
Searching for its echo
An emotional shrimp
With his heart in his head
A teaspoon of a neutron star
Weighing more than the human population
Everything important
And all things we'd never imagine
How small do you feel now?

Abby Carey (15)
Fairfield High School for Girls, Droylsden

What's It To Us?

They say that it's impossible to sneeze with open eyes
That there could be one billion stars lighting up the skies
That only chimps can recognise themselves when in a mirror
That crocodiles swallow stones to help them dive deeper
There are 86,400 seconds crammed into just one day
For twenty-eight minutes underwater an iguana it can stay

But what's the use of this to us?
How could they be so sad?
To sit and calculate these things
They must be going mad!

Charlotte Knowles (16)
Fairfield High School for Girls, Droylsden

Spectre In The Shadows

With teeth as hard as steel
And eyes that burn like fire,
I wade amongst the darkness
My fins they never tire.

Patrolling deep blue seas
With nothing in my way,
I hover through the coral
And pass a stinging ray.

I'm perceived as a monster
One no one wants to meet,
I don't mean to harm anyone
But I have to kill to eat!

You'll see me in the movies
I've worked my way to fame,
I even have my own theme tune
I'm sure you know my name.

Abigail Murray (15)
Fairfield High School for Girls, Droylsden

A Man's Best Friend

An enemy to the garden
eating all the flowers
running round and round
jumping up and down.

Standing so tall
with his bright beady eyes
his soft, soft fur
and cheeky smile.

Like a big, furry teddy
who plays all day
no time for sleep
just play, play, play.

Leaping round the house
running round the table
jumping on the sofas
scratching on the door!

Danielle Bateson (11)
Flixton Girls' High School, Urmston

Friends

Friends are great, they're important to me,
Friends are for life, not just for tea.
Friends are always there for you,
Friends need you to be there too.
Friends go through some times which are sad,
Friends would *never* break up for a lad.
Friends are funny, friends are kind,
Friends help you make up your mind.
If you have a true friend for life,
Don't let them go, it's like being stabbed with a knife.

Hannah Mackenzie (11)
Flixton Girls' High School, Urmston

Elliot

When Elliot passed away,
There was no happiness in my life.
People crying, people sad,
No happiness in my life.
Tubes all over him,
No happiness in my life.
Letting go slowly,
No happiness in my life.
Holding a cold baby boy,
No happiness in my life.
Cremated to ashes,
No happiness in my life.
But the best thing to remember; he
Was my brother,
Happiness of a memory.

Natalie Price (11)
Flixton Girls' High School, Urmston

Love

Love is the thing you need the most,
Whether it's family or friends, lovers too,
They are all someone that's special to you.
Love is something to share,
It's something that's fair,
It means a lot to me,
Because I can see,
Without love you're nowhere.
Love is to care,
Love makes me smile,
Love is something that lasts for a while.
Love is here, love is there,
Hey, love is everywhere.

Hannah MacDonald (11)
Flixton Girls' High School, Urmston

Pink

Pink is the colour just for me,
Loving, styling and everyone can see.

Pink is the colour that I like,
Pink is the colour of my bike.

Pink is the colour of my cheeks,
Pink is the colour when my heart speaks.

Pink is the colour when I blush,
Pink is the colour when I see my crush!

Pink is the colour just for me,
Pink is the colour for me, everyone can see.

Abbey Whittaker (11)
Flixton Girls' High School, Urmston

Jack Frost

Jack Frost comes with an evil grin,
He vanishes off in a spin.

Jack Frost comes with a stick and a case,
The trees shout, 'Did you see the smirk on his face?'

The jagged javelins drop on the floor,
The meadows shout, 'I don't want any more.'

Wherever you look there is crystal-white,
Not a thing left that is bold or bright.

The trees are chattering with fear,
As Jack Frost shouts, 'I am here!'

To finish Frost heat him up,
Take the juice out and drink it in a teacup.

Tayaba Hussain (12)
Flixton Girls' High School, Urmston

Toffee, Toffee, My Little Rabbit

Toffee, Toffee, I love Toffee,
Toffee, Toffee, my little rabbit.
Toffee, Toffee, he hates carrots,
Toffee, Toffee, loves lettuce and cabbage.
Toffee, Toffee, my little rabbit,
Toffee, Toffee, loves the outdoors.
Toffee, Toffee, my little rabbit!

Katie Parker (11)
Flixton Girls' High School, Urmston

Christmas Poem

Snow is everywhere, it's all I see
A white blanket so crisp, so delicate
I am so glad to be inside on this special day
Surrounded by people I know and love
Opening presents and having fun
The smell of the Christmas dinner
Makes your mouth water.

Chelsea Brown (12)
Flixton Girls' High School, Urmston

Winter

Winter is here
Her icy fingers reached out to all the trees,
She grabbed them and pulled off their leaves
Then she covered the streets with snow
Went to the sun and dimmed its glow
She took the fields and buried them in ice
People built her snowmen, only the best would suffice
And from the skies hail did fall
No creature big or creature small
Could escape Winter's cold cruel wrath
It was then that she did laugh
At all the plants' and animals' distress
For when they suffered she could not care less.

Shauna Brown (12)
Flixton Girls' High School, Urmston

Music . . .

All the instruments all over the world,
Some are square, some are curled.

Guitars with strings, triangles ting,
Drums that bang, cymbals clang.

The pitch of the music can be low,
But it can be quite high though.

Boom, boom, bang, clash, clash, clang,
It can be squeaky as well as creaky.

When you listen to the beat,
Sometimes you want to tap your feet.

Liz Loss (12)
Flixton Girls' High School, Urmston

Stars

I look up to the stars,
They're dancing for me,
When you look up to the stars,
It's easy to see.

All my fears and worries seem to run away,
With the glistening night
The stars are dancing, shining bright
Oh how many stories they tell
When I see their shapes
It makes me feel swell
The sparkling stars guide me
With the moon as their king
The stars are dancing, as I sing
The stars are dancing
Dancing for me
When you look up to the sky, you can see.

Christie Ronaldson (12)
Flixton Girls' High School, Urmston

My Babysitter

She sent me to bed again,
She's being a real pain.
She said I'm too young to stay up past eight,
I was twelve last week for heaven's sake.
She unplugs my telly and takes my phone,
Says I can have 'em tomorrow when Mum and Dad are home.
She invites him round like it's her house,
I feel like saying get lost or get out.
I sit in the dark and listen to giggles,
I get so bored I get the wriggles.
My mum and dad know I hate her,
They should call a different operator.
I bet there's nicer people than her,
Who play with you, stay with you, not treat you like dirt.
I hate her so much I wish she would go,
It's a good job the payment is low.
Well her name's Nancy and she's so bitter
And she's my evil babysitter!

Kate Roberts (12)
Flixton Girls' High School, Urmston

Home Sweet Home

The warm scent as you open the door,
Even the walls and the floor,
The roaring fire,
Which people admire,
The spitting flames which are so neat,
Give off a terrific heat,
So sit back and relax
And enjoy the comfort of home.

Katie Langford (12)
Flixton Girls' High School, Urmston

Winter Wizard

The autumn leaves have fallen down
But now the winter wizard
Sweeps across the world with his snowy gown
A wave of his wand, the world will freeze
And comes with this a winter breeze
The trees are stiff and sadly bare
But the winter wizard, he doesn't care!
Soon ice and snow will cover the earth
It's just like winter has given birth
Icicles hang from rooftops
But the winter wizard
He never stops
He has been trapped all year round
But to people's fear he has been found
The birds will flee
He smiles with glee
Children will play day to day
But soon the winter wizard will say
You must go and with this snow. . .
He cast a curse upon the world!

Charlotte Haskins (12)
Flixton Girls' High School, Urmston

Spring Spiral!

Tiny seeds coiled, waiting for the sun to warm the earth.
Daffodils with bent heads,
Dance gracefully in the spring breeze.
The twisted hazel catkins hang like lambs' tails.
Aminals emerge from hibernation,
Spring, coil, sprout, shoot,
Germinate, loop, curl, entwine, roll, twirl, wind . . . spring!

Claire Duckett (13)
Flixton Girls' High School, Urmston

Paxos Holiday

I wish I was back in that crystal clear sea,
You by my side eating Souvalanki,
Sitting by the pool, just you and me,
Feeling such a fool for getting panicky,
Everything we did just fell into place,
Apart from that maze,
I can remember your face,
I hope we go to Paxos one day,
Laugh like we did on our last holiday,
The days on the boat with Helen and Mark,
Finding that lagoon,
Swimming under that arch.

Ashley Wild (12)
Flixton Girls' High School, Urmston

Getting Up

Alarm clock goes,
Time to get up!
Wash my face to wake me up.
Next get dressed,
Listening to the radio.
Go downstairs to have my breakfast,
With a drink of orange juice.
Back upstairs,
Clean my teeth,
Brush my hair, no time to spare.
Check my bag, everything's packed,
In the car driving to school.
Getting out, 'Bye Mum, love you.'
Into school to see my friends,
That's my morning routine.

Katie Jackson (13)
Flixton Girls' High School, Urmston

My Secret Hideout

My secret hideout is high in a tree
I go there every day to play
Just my best friend and me.

We play all sorts of games
Like pirates out at sea
Or make up funny names
Just my best friend and me.

My brother tries to come and play
But we say no you see
And then we send him away
Just my best friend and me.

We play all day but then Mum calls
Now it's time for tea
So we jump down from the tree so tall
Just my best friend and me.

Sophie Brown (12)
Flixton Girls' High School, Urmston

Friendship

A friend is somebody who is special,
A friend should always be grateful,
A friend is known as a mate,
A mate who you should never ever hate.

A friend should always be sharing,
Someone who is always caring.
A friend should be close to your heart,
Even if they are far apart.

Sometimes times can get tough
And friends can seem a bit rough
But always remember, that friends are forever
And all friends should stick together - forever!

Asma Hafesji (12)
Flixton Girls' High School, Urmston

Rainy Day!

Rain comes down, soaks the ground,
People rushing all around,
Umbrellas up, sun hats down,
Feeling like you're getting drowned.

Wishing you were far away,
On a magical holiday,
Fingers like icicles, feet like snow,
You are drenched from head to toe.

Rain comes down, soaks the ground,
People rushing all around,
Umbrellas up, sun hats down,
Feeling like you're getting drowned.

Cathy Estkowski (12)
Flixton Girls' High School, Urmston

Wakey Wakey!

Wake with the ticking of the alarm clock,
Tick-tock, tick-tock.
I get dressed ready for school,
Telling Mother to keep her cool.
Brush my raggily hair,
Almost as tough as a bear.
Gobble my cornflakes,
Whilst waiting for the pastries to bake.
Grab my lunch box,
Steal a spoon of my sister's Coco Rocks.
Get in the car,
Watching I don't whack my head on the bar.
Now I'm at school,
Ready to learn,
The bells ring,
A-ring-a-ding-ding.

Ashlea Hutton (13)
Flixton Girls' High School, Urmston

Help the Homeless

The homeless are people too
They're unhappier than me or you
They look forward to this time of year
That's the Booth Centre coming near
We donate to make them feel good
And it's nice to know they have grub
All I'm saying is donate some money
Or fruit or jam or even honey.

We need to help the hungry
But don't give anything gungy
Some people aren't nice
They see them in ice
And frankly just don't care.

Charlotte McPhee (13)
Flixton Girls' High School, Urmston

Going To Bed

My mummy said, 'Time for bed,'
And I ran away.

She made me a bath
So I jumped in and got her soaking wet.

I washed my hair
And cleaned my teeth and played with my toys.

Mummy said, 'Come on, time's up,'
But I shooed her away.

I got bored and jumped out the bath
And ran about the room.

My mummy came in and told me off
And made me clean the room.

I was good and did what I was told
I finished and shouted, 'I'm outta here.'

I zoomed down the stairs and found my mum
And told her I wanted a story.

Of course I didn't hear the end
I was asleep as mummy would say
'Time for bed.'

Victoria Gillespie (12)
Flixton Girls' High School, Urmston

Winter!

Winter is the season to be jolly
So deck the halls with bows of holly.

Snow makes a blanket all over the land
Fir trees catch it like green hands.

Slip and slide all over the ice
Snowflakes fall overnight.

Plants and animals hide away
On the cold and dreadful days.

Gabrielle Williams (12)
Flixton Girls' High School, Urmston

Pollution!

I look out my window
and what do I see?
A glorious picture of red
blue and green.
But all of this glory
will soon be a story
with a sense of 'solution'
that we call pollution!
The animals, people, plants and sea
is what the beautiful world used to be.
If we keep repeating
the planet's mistreating
the colours and sound will soon be gone
for what we are doing is definitely *wrong.*

Rachael Hilton (12)
Flixton Girls' High School, Urmston

Hanged

He enters the room broad and tall,
As the night begins to fall,
He tells his daughter it will all be OK
And they will see each other again some other day.

They take him to a whole new place,
He knows he's not safe.
They explain clearly for the sin he commited with a knife,
He now has to pay with his life.

He begins to panic with fright in his heart,
Will his daughter ever forgive him for murdering Mark?
Mark was his friend, his son in need,
Now they both have to pay for that awful deed.

Walking up the gallows bare, he begins to weep,
In his mind he knows his daughter is safe in bed, fast asleep.
With a rope round his neck and his arms in cuffs,
His legs tied up and his face all muffed.

The gates open, his fingers clench,
This is it, the time is here,
Old farmer Joe is going to get hanged . . .
With his eyes filled with fear!

Miriam Khan (12)
Flixton Girls' High School, Urmston

Sweetie!

I've got a sweetie, I'm giving it away,
It's been in my pocket for more than one day,
It's got no wrapper,
It's covered in fluff,
Would you like my sweetie?
No! I've had enough.

All my friends have sucked it
And so has my gran,
My daddy found it in the back of his van,
My uncle Malc didn't like it so he spat it out,
Would you like my sweetie?
No! I'm havin' nowt.

Georgia Oldfield (12)
Flixton Girls' High School, Urmston

I Met?

I met?
I'm cold and I'm tired
My eyes are tearful and my nose is blocked
I am wearing a scarf, hat and gloves
Along with my big coat, pockets full of tissues
I am walking as slow as a snail
So cold I can barely move
I wish I could curl up in my living room
On my sofa with the fire blazing and my pyjamas
And dressing gown wrapped tightly around me
Making me feel safe and cosy
And at night the Christmas tree lights on
The heating on, watching my favourite soaps
Unravelling a chocolate in the shape of a man
Wearing a big red coat and pants and shiny shoes and a beard
But it's soon over, the leaves are back on the trees
My eyes start to water
But I'll be back next year I promise
What am I?

A: winter.

Holly Thorne (12)
Flixton Girls' High School, Urmston

Cats

Playful and giddy until their next nap,
Chasing wool like they chase mice,
Lying in the sun and falling asleep,
Fur shining in the sun, some silky, some fluffy.

If you stroke them they will purr
And miaow for their dinner,
Going in and out through your legs,
Waiting impatiently for their food,
They lick milk up with their little pink tongue.

They have little eyes which shine at night,
They hunt around for mice in the dark,
On sunny days they will pounce around,
Trying to catch pretty butterflies.

Jessica Harper (12)
Flixton Girls' High School, Urmston

Toes

One toe, two toes, three toes, four,
Five toes, six toes, seven toes, more.
Big toes, little toes,
Toes aren't really a bore.

After a long day
With toes at work,
They start
To really hurt.

My toes are
Attached to my feet,
So they get cold
When walking in the street.

I keep my toes warm
By putting them in socks,
I keep them warm
So I don't get chickenpox.

One toe, two toes, three toes, four,
Five toes, six toes, seven toes, more.
Now you know
Toes aren't a bore.

Sophie Stedman (12)
Flixton Girls' High School, Urmston

My Favourite Things

Shopping

I like shopping for clothes, bags and shoes
And all the little things like bracelets and perfume.
I shop, shop, shop till I drop
Or until it's time for the shops to shut.

Bounce

It's big, it's round
And the colour is blue
I can bounce on my own
Or can bounce with you
It's tiring but it's fun
It's hard to believe
It's my trampoline.

Swimming

Swimming in the pool
Swimming in the sea
Backstroke, breaststroke
It's all the same to me
Diving, jumping
But do not run
It could save your life as well as having fun.

TV

I like TV
TV likes me
I would watch it all day
But my parents disagree
I'd go to the cinema every day
But my mum's that tight she won't even pay.

Holly Turner (11)
Flixton Girls' High School, Urmston

It's Hallowe'en Night

On a spooky Hallowe'en night
When goblins and witches come out to fright
They knock at your door
Should you open it?
Should you be scared?
Trick or treaters are everywhere
It's only one day
One night in fact
It's Hallowe'en night.

Don't go out on Hallowe'en night
Stay in your bed and keep on the light
Little demons have their fun alright
Outside on the streets on Hallowe'en night.

Green eyes with their mysterious stare
Black cats are sure to scare
As witches fly I count my sweets
Everyone's still out there on Hallowe'en night.

Lantern burning bright
Still the moon keeps shining bright
Darkness comes to make it night
Children given a fright on Hallowe'en night.

Katie Silgram (12)
Flixton Girls' High School, Urmston

My Clever Kitty

Oh kitty what is it like to hold?
It's in the sky
Something you cannot touch,
Pull it down,
Or wrap it up tight,
Like a little bird who longs to be free
You cannot hold it,
Or wrap it up tight,
It just sits up there,
Like a diamond in the night.

Oh kitty, oh kitty,
Why can't we?
Because it belongs up there in the big blue sea
As with all stars for you to see.

Lucy Isabella Williams (11)
Flixton Girls' High School, Urmston

Autumn Is Here

The moon glistens white over the land,
The fearless beasts cower in the hills,

The leaves of the trees dance with the wind,
The pumpkins grow, in full flourish

Ready for Hallowe'en, the night draws near
Droplets of dew hang on the grass.

The night cries out for colour, attention,
The blacks and the browns, the sunshine

Longed, but for now, the cloudy canopy
Above the world, lingers there awhile.

Then drifts away for the angels' tears
To grace the land, the plants sulk away.

Autumn is here.

Shaun Brown (14)
Fred Longworth High School, Tyldesley

Passport Poem

My name, Rose from the Hay Meadows.

My nationality is the home of fish and chips.

I had hope when I was born.
I am as small as a doll and am as light as a feather,
Floating down from a bird and softly touching down on the earth.

My nails are daggers, as long as a cat's.
My long hair is medium brown with natural blonde streaks.
No one has, or ever will, have my colour of hair,
It's one of my best features, a feature that no one owns

My eyes are hazel and are as shiny as a diamond.
I can express my feelings well.

I am not yet famous but I am building up to be.
I am my own unique self when all is deserted,
But in front of everyone else I am a different person,
obviously not me!

Hayley Clarkson (12)
Fred Longworth High School, Tyldesley

My Passport Poem

When the day begins I open my fiery eyes
As the sunbeams rise slowly as I awake.

From the bangers and mash citizenship spirit of Great Britain
I have a burning love for chips and pies
I am a Briton at heart, a British bulldog I am!

Rushed away to a shut-down ruin
Born in broken glass and gravel
Well that's what left of Billinge hospital
Where my amazing life began.

I am as bold and as strong as a mountain
And yet as tall as one as well
I take after my statuesque mother.

My weight is anonymous to me, I think I am average for my age
Even though I am so totally unaverage in . . .
Everything else!

I have golden hair that forms itself into a little hedge around my head
My family call me Goldilocks,
Is it a compliment?

Lucy Aspinall (11)
Fred Longworth High School, Tyldesley

Identity Poem

Name: I was a born leader
Leader of anyone.

Height: I am as tall as a newborn giraffe.

Weight: I weigh half as much as my dad.

Nationality: I was born in the land of fish and chips
And the inventor of the pound.

POB: I was born in the land of the pie-eater
The underdogs of football
In Billinge Hospital I was born.

Distinguishing marks: I am as white as the driven snow
I can be recognised by my freckles
Or my golden hazel eyes.

Martyn Parkinson (12)
Fred Longworth High School, Tyldesley

Passport Poem

Christ helper, coming forth, helping weary travellers,
From the land of hope and glory.
Born with hope in my heart.
Home of fish and chips and the pie.
That's the place I was born and proud I am for sure.
I am as bold as a rock and as sturdy as a tree,
Swaying in the north wind.
The scar on my head caused by the sea of the whale
And the cuts on my legs caused from me swinging through the trees.

Chris Howard (11)
Fred Longworth High School, Tyldesley

Identity Poem

Name: Protector of man, bold and strong.
Full of wisdom am I.

Nationality: Home of the penny, land of the sausage and mash.

Place of birth: Born in a ward, love and joy surrounds me
as I'm welcomed to the world.

Height: Not as tall as a tower, not as small as an ant,
I am the middle man.

Weight: Big like a bull, a lump of power and strength.

Distinguishing marks: Hands big like a tiger.

Alexander Whitworth (12)
Fred Longworth High School, Tyldesley

Passport Poem

My name is the day's eve,
Glowing in the afternoon sun.

I come from the town,
That is the place of the pits.

Born in the hospital of hope,
Shining, happy and bright.

I'm as tall as a 4x4 Jeep,
Standing tall in the road.

As heavy as lead,
Big and bold.

I can coax a beautiful piece of music.

Daisy Lummis (11)
Fred Longworth High School, Tyldesley

Identity Poem

Name: I'm a fruity as a fig, the place where miracles happen.

Live: Stretching my fruitylious eyes wide open,
Looking at the view of people, football, football is life!

Birthplace: Born in Billinge Hospital,
Overlooking the fields of the north-west,
High upon those hills.

Nationality: Underneath the George Cross of the England flag.

Height: Being as tall as a tree and as colourful as a yellow rose.

Weight: Light as a feather flying round the streets of my home town.

Distinguishing mark: I'm just me.

Beth Berry (11)
Fred Longworth High School, Tyldesley

Passport Poem

Name: Universal, of the world,
Meaning I keep the world in its complete whole.

Nationality: My nationality is the place where the British bulldog
is homed
And the place where the famous fish and chips are produced.

Birthplace: The Hope for Salford and times to come in the heart
of Salford,
A famous place to bring people into the world.

Height: Maybe as big as a car,
Or maybe even I could be a little tree
When autumn has hit it and the leaves have fallen to the ground.

Weight: My weight is like a sack of feathers (wrapped round a sack
of house bricks).
In the middle of the different weights, not bigger, not smaller.

Distinguishing marks: I have strawberry blonde hair,
It is quite straight but sometimes curls in places.

Emma Greenall (11)
Fred Longworth High School, Tyldesley

Passport Poem

Name: A Hebrew bound and tied, followed by 'the victorious one'.

DOB: The second day of the second month, the month of love when Cupid aims his arrows for the unsuspecting lovers.

Place of birth: The home of Manchester United, the best team in the world.

Nationality: From a lovely small island, a beautiful place to live.

Height: As tall as a jumping dolphin on a beautiful blue sea.

Weight: I am like a baby elephant, heavy but cuddly.

Distinguishing marks: My eyes are as brown as a female blackbird.

Rebecka Jayne Stevens (13)
Fred Longworth High School, Tyldesley

That Girl

On my own,
Out on the streets,
Memories of a good home,
Yet memories of abuse.

I sit alone,
Watching life pass by,
People look at me laughing,
Nobody helps me.

I'm only 15,
I shouldn't be here,
Drowning in my sorrows,
Wishing to be at school.

When my mother died,
That's when it started,
No help from my family,
No hope of friends.

Nothing hurts more than the hatred,
Lack of love
And hardship,
That is my life.

I want to die,
No point in living,
No hope of a future,
No hope of help.

On my own,
Out on the streets,
Memories of a good home,
Yet memories of abuse.

Heather Wilkinson (13)
Fred Longworth High School, Tyldesley

Why Me?

You make me cry, you make me hurt,
You laugh at me like I am dirt,

You feed me threats, you give me fears,
I always have to hide my tears,

Your comments ring inside my head,
I've took in every word you've said,

You make me feel like I am wrong,
You've picked on me for far too long,

I feel afraid, so insecure,
Each act cuts deeper than the one before,

Why me? I find I contemplate,
Am I resigned to accept my fate?

With nowhere to run, with nowhere to hide,
I need someone by my side.

Sian Gilfillan (11)
Fred Longworth High School, Tyldesley

My Season Of Joy

Oh wonderful winter,
With your bed of frost
And your cool droplets of snow.

You bring us the snowmen,
You give us the snowballs
And you are the season for me.

Every year I see you making angels in the snow,
Watching the falling of flakes,
Listening to the crispness of the ice.

You are my season of joy.

Thomas Berry (14)
Fred Longworth High School, Tyldesley

Evacuation

The air raid sirens sound again,
Deafening, angry, blaring
Above is the drone of German bombers
Where the soldiers sit, staring

Children panic, run, scream,
I cling to Mother's arm
For what may be the final time;
Tomorrow, I'll be safe from harm . . .

I latch onto my mother's hand,
For soon I'll be alone
Evacuee, my ticket screams
Destination: *unknown.*

Hours later, I arrive,
Where? I do not know,
A man, he spots my name tag, snarls,
'Hurry then, let's go!'

For many months I stay outdoors
Inside I'm glared at hard
I feel unwanted, until one night
A shadow creeps on the yard.

I run out to investigate,
The intruder by the barns
Suddenly, I'm racing, sobbing . . .
Into my mother's arms.

She's hugging me so tightly,
I know she's missed me so,
'Darling, now I've found you, I
Will never let you go.'

Beth Allison (12)
Heworth Grange Comprehensive School, Gateshead

My World Of Chocolate!

Chocolate, what a wonderful thing,
Cadbury's, their name has such a ring,
A Flake, Dairy Milk or even a Twirl,
They make the saliva in my mouth go *Swirl!*

What about Galaxy, it tastes so yummy,
That chocolatey badness that fills up your tummy,
Keep it for a sleepover, if you like to share,
But don't let it melt cos it'll go everywhere!

There are loads of types of chocolate, from Penzance to Bombay,
Kinder Bueno, Twix and Time Out, Rocky and Milky Way,
Hot in a mug, or solid in a bar,
Both sold in shops, near or far!

Chocolate is such a fabulous food, I could eat it all day long,
My dad says I should cut out the chocolate . . . er . . . wrong!
Chocolate is what is beautiful about our little world,
Celebrating the fact that . . . well . . . chocolate rules the world!

Don't pay any attention to the people who're on a diet,
They say they don't want any, then eat it on the quiet,
Spending all their money on the chocolatey stuff,
Eating and eating, they just can't get enough!

You know what's really yummy? Chocolate spread on toast,
That's my favourite breakfast, that's what I like the most,
I also love the yoghurts made with Cadbury's Flakes,
And the cakes you can get from Greggs, the mini chocolate cakes!

Chocolate is my life and chocolate is my love,
I hope you all agree with what I've written above.
I completely adore chocolate from my head down to my toes,
I would definitely love to live where a cocoa tree grows!

Alice Thompson (12)
Heworth Grange Comprehensive School, Gateshead

Autumn Is Near

Autumn is near, summer days are gone
crisp leaves flutter amidst the woods
crunching beneath my numb feet, buried inside
boots of worn leather.

The dying branches of broken trees,
curl towards me hauntingly
hidden behind the smoke and mirrors that conceal us
like a broken heart torn beneath us.

Harsh cold wind whips my fresh face, giving no mercy,
remains of the fleshy fruit of autumn, lies untouched
upon the muddy forest floor.
Nothing but illusion remains here,
autumn is near, summer days are gone.

A crack of a twig is sounded in the distance
creeping up on me through what's left.
Still I must continue, ignore the rest,
continue my walk through the woods.

I step into the clearing, finally seeing
the world through my own eyes
just disappear from the world,
like the leaves from now bare trees,
autumn is near, summer days are gone.

Amina Jamil (12)
Parrs Wood High School, East Didsbury

Sarah's House

My friend Sarah asked me over for the very first time,
I wondered what her house would be like and if it was rather fine.
I met her mum at the end of the day, to check if it was okay.
I ran home and told my mum who was looking rather glum,
She said fine, as long as I don't whine about it all the time.

On the way I sang a song which sounded very wrong but I didn't care
as long as we got there.
I knocked on the door with a smile on my face
that no one could ever trace.
I walked into the hall which was as grand as a Mall.
We sat down for dinner, which I could see wasn't going to make
me any thinner.
It seemed like their house was a trace of the Queen's place.
Sarah's room was great, because of it, she's now my best mate.
In the morning we played games which were about fame.
At lunch I had to get my stuff so I left in a huff.
If only I could dine . . . one last time!

Connie Ross (11)
Parrs Wood High School, East Didsbury

In The Past

Her eyes like beetroot, from lack of a comfy bed,
her cheeks rosy apples, beaming though freezing.
Her smile like a sun that lights up people's lives,
her name is Ethel and as it would suggest,
a decent old woman is she, though with a horrible past.

Her past is long and treacherous, to say bad would
be an insult.
Her mum and dad were alcoholics, abused her
yes they did.
A good child she was, just unfortunate, her parents
of the 'smacking' cult.
Her name is Ethel and as it would suggest, a decent
old woman is she, with a horrible past.

Her future is uncertain, a toddler amongst mist,
she takes every day as it comes, she knows it could be her last.
Of all the bad things that have happened to her,
longer than a Christmas list.
Her name is Ethel and as it would suggest, a decent old woman is she,
though with a horrible past.

Katie Paterson
Parrs Wood High School, East Didsbury

Alfred

His face is long and thin
but nothing compared to his chin.
It's the shape of a boiled egg
and his name is Alfred.
His eyes are always hiding
and never seem to be widening.
He's been old since the year ahead
and his name is Alfred.

His life has been as dark as a dungeon
and the woman of his life has gone.
Their little baby daughter is dead,
who was murdered by him, Alfred.
And now he has joined the army
he must have been barmy.
He hates being around the living and dead
and his name is Alfred.

Naomi Stark (11)
Parrs Wood High School, East Didsbury

From Vampire To Sensation

She has a sad look on her face,
She has jet-black hair,
She has eyes that chill you to the bone,
She has blood dripping down her chin,
She has a mansion in the south of Transylvania,
She lives off your blood.

When she was a little girl,
Her mum loved her to death,
She used to be happy,
She used to enjoy herself
But then someone shot her mum,
And now she's mad at the world.
She sleeps all day,
She hunts all night,
Looking for someone to feast on,
Trying to find her mum,
Trying to live again.

Then one day she woke up and she didn't feel hungry,
She didn't feel like hunting,
She didn't feel like killing,
Instead, she felt like singing,
Getting up on stage and having the time of her life.

From that day on, she didn't kill,
She didn't want to be like the man that killed her mum,
She wanted to have people listen to her music,
And hear them sing along when they heard it,
And that's just what she did.

Robyn Callagan (12)
Parrs Wood High School, East Didsbury

The Wolf At The Door

The sky bled, hell-fire red, burnt
pulsing threads of the sunset
dooming, bombing, night draws in
and the wolves are at the door.

I sit, stung by what was said -
phone rings. Screaming down the line,
we spit barbs and hornet stings
and the wolves are at the door.

Okay, shouldn't have, but did,
we snarled like mongrels, needling,
caustered half-healed sores and tears
and the wolves are at the door.

So I brood alone in the gloom,
reaping what we've sown. Guilt
curdles sour, molten bile in my guts.
Maybe I should -

What's that?
What's that slinking shadow,
passing the beam of the streetlight?
What's that slow scratch on wood?

Haven't you guessed?

Lorna Petty (15)
Parrs Wood High School, East Didsbury

The Misfortunate Bride!

Ellen Egweeny Eggwood was the name of the misfortunate bride,
To others she seemed so happy, with a large smile across
                                                her round face,
But to the ones that saw her deep, could see that she was drowning
                                                in her sorrows,
From her pale skin, the others knew she longed to be somewhere else.
Her silky brown hair, tied with a lace, shone in the summer sun.
Her marble-white teeth glowed in the eyes of many.
Her eyes were like small fishes in the deep blue sea,
The sea in her eyes was the tears that she feared.

The bride's glistening eye glared at her guest,
This wedding, she knew was going to leave her life in a quest!
Her dad was a drug dealer,
Who made her life end in failure.
At the age of three, she had lost her mother,
She had never seen the sight of a school,
For that poor girl, her experience was high but education was low.
She was abused and refused so many times,
That she started to believe the only escape was suicide.

Today was the day she was to be wed to a man, who she had
                                                never met.
This wedding, she knew was going to leave her life in a quest!
Who he was, she did not know,
Where he was from, she did not know,
How he looked, she did not know.
She knew nothing but the fact that she would be free from her
                                                dreadful father,
Her future lies with many mysteries and suspense.

Thurkka Rajeswaran (13)
Parrs Wood High School, East Didsbury

The Evil School Bell

Cold blood runs through my veins,
As the time of fear reigns.
The thought of being without my mum,
Sends butterflies flying around my tum.
As terror draws ever near,
My mum says, 'Time for school dear,'
As I enter the ground of Hell,
I hear the sound of the morning bell,
And as I walk down the corridor,
My feeling of fear rises ever more.
And when I arrive, I feel a fool,
As there really is nothing wrong with school.

Nathan Harvey Jones (11)
Parrs Wood High School, East Didsbury

The Wedding Day!

Her face looks happy from far away as she puts on her bridal veil,
But look deep inside her close-set eyes and you will
see they're full of sorrow.
Her long black hair pulled tightly back, fastened with a flowery clip,
And however hard she tries to smile, it makes her face bleaker.

She looks back to the question asked, which she had to answer,
Too shocked to speak, too shocked to answer
her father steps in for her,
However much he hates her and how much she hates him back,
He will not let go of this, he never would at that.

Her aunty sits in the audience waiting for the bride,
And as she passes by her, what a beautiful sight,
Red roses for eternal love are clutched in her trembling hands
Silver shoes with pointed tips walk forward to the altar.

Her new husband waits for her at the altar, a golden ring in one hand,
She steps up onto the platform where their vows are said,
Now only one word left to say, how hard can one word be?
Looking into his sparkling eyes, a whole new world she can see.

Emotion grips her suddenly as she holds out her hand,
'Yes!' is spoken lightly but you can see that she's glad,
She knows that this is the end, her future set and ready,
But looking into those sparkling eyes, who could miss this chance?

Louise Tattershall (12)
Parrs Wood High School, East Didsbury

No Gun For Asmir

The country of Bosnia was in uproar,
Soldiers went out determined,
Returned at death's door
And Asmir's young face was smiling no more,
He looked so forlorn as his tears hit the floor.

A shortage of food,
And families split up.
Every friend was a foe
Every neighbour a crook.

A frightening noise,
A dark smell of fire.
A crackle of flames,
Like a funeral pyre.

The blaze all but engulfed him,
No place left to hide.
His heart sank within him,
He was breaking inside.
Then Asmir's young face was crying no more,
Because Asmir was lying, dead on the floor.

Josie Throup (11)
Parrs Wood High School, East Didsbury

A Big Disgrace

His name's Bob Cally, he's 38,
and looks a big disgrace,
he's got muddy and scarred skin
with an ugly chin.

An overgrown moustache and beard,
his eyes are bright brown like a coconut,
with a banana-shaped head,
he's had a tragic life.

His past ended with a blast,
he lost his wife and son
in a bomb explosion,
no wonder, his biggest fear is kids,
he drinks and drinks till he sinks in a river of tears.

No one knows what the future holds,
Alcoholic and lives in a box,
I'm sure he'll get eaten by a fox.

Amy Moss (13)
Parrs Wood High School, East Didsbury

Poem Odyssey

A poem brings bright joy
Like a loud child with a toy

A poem is like a fast train
On a long, long chain

Or like a long car
Driving along a nightclub bar

A poem is like a song
But not as long

A poem can make you angry like war
Or could be a bore

A poem could be zest
If it's one of the best

And if you've been dreaming, a poem will never make sense.

Matthew Graham (14)
St Aidan's County High School, Carlisle

A Poem Odyssey!

A poem fills you with joy,
like a child playing with a toy.

A poem is a story cut short,
in a lesson waiting to be taught.

A poem is a way to describe,
they give off a great vibe.

A poem is bursting with rhyme,
it happens all the time.

A poem has a fast-beating flow,
inside it makes you glow.

A poem is incredibly snappy,
it makes you feel really happy.

A poem rips through your mind like fire,
it spins round like a car tyre.

Laura Plunkett (14)
St Aidan's County High School, Carlisle

A Poem Is . . .

A poem is like a song
s . . . l . . . o . . . w . . . e . . . d down,
Like a gale force wind
dying down to a swift breeze.

A poem entertains the reader
like a clown at a circus.
Juggling, slipping and then f
                              a
                              l
                               l
                                i
                                 n
                                  g (crash!)
to the ground.

A poem is like a short tale
giving mixed emotions,
Like a boy with a lolly
tumbling and grazing his knees.

A poem makes the reader imagine,
like the wild imagination of a young girl
with the imaginary friends she's found.

A poem is like a jigsaw
coming together piece by piece.
Like a broken vase that fell
accidentally off the mantelpiece.

A poem can make you weep
like when your mum couldn't *s-t-o-p*
and she ran over your three-month-old kitten.

A poem may use metaphors or can drop
in a simile like the rain flying in through
an open window, and being as cold as ice!

Tanya Foster (14)
St Aidan's County High School, Carlisle

Poem Odyssey

A poem is like a story book
full of twists, turns and ideas.
A blazing flame of woeful thoughts or
ice crystals of joyful ideas.
A poem sometimes rhymes a lot.
Uses similes to help it fly.
It's a window to the writer's soul,
A door to the writer's ideas.
You can use metaphors, connotations or rhyming words.
It's a melody with a tune you really
need to hear!
It's like a bird flying free with your emotions
resting on its wings.
Gliding and rhyming with its wings and
words filled with your ideas, hopeful and weird.
It's like a man standing on a roof shouting your words,
Making my head stop and think of the word.
It's in your thoughts and hopes and a wonderful idea is
hopeful or weird, whatever you feel!
So pick up your pencil and paper and think of some words
and tell your story to the rest of the world.

Katie Burns (14)
St Aidan's County High School, Carlisle

A Poem Is . . .

Poems are like Calpol
They can make you feel better.

Poems are like jets,
They can go fast.

Poems are like snails,
They can go slow.

Poems are like little brothers,
They are annoying.

Callum Braithwaite (14)
St Aidan's County High School, Carlisle

My Poem

A poem, hmm a poem!
Well a poem has lots of things

Like a table tennis bat
when it hits a ball and
p . . . i . . . n . . . g . . . s!

A poem can also be very excruciating
but it can be excellent for a wealthy king.

A poem cannot go on forever,
like a very light floating feather.

A poem gets boring after a while
like a bathroom tile.

Now I'm going to go away because
I haven't got anything else to say.

Callum Irving (14)
St Aidan's County High School, Carlisle

Poem Odyssey

A poem is a short story
That tells you tales in a rhythm.

A poem can be bought
And then it can be taught.

A poem can tell crimes
A poem sometimes rhymes.

A poem is told by a clown
That is a song slowed down.

A poem sometimes has a devotion
But certainly lots of emotion
And also lots of commotion.

A poem is like a happy day
That makes you want to play.

A poem is like a baby
That fills you full of joy, maybe!

Amy Chandler (14)
St Aidan's County High School, Carlisle

A Poem Odyssey

A poem is a story,
marching through mixed feelings.

A poem has heaps of emotions
and can send a chill down your spine.

A poem can swarm you with sorrow
or fill you up with joy.

A poem can be confusing
or easy to understand.

A poem can be set in space
or be set in school, or your personal place.

A poem should really make you think,
like why is there an elephant in the kitchen sink?

Whatever poem you wish to read
it should be fun and exciting indeed.

Amy Nelson (14)
St Aidan's County High School, Carlisle

A Poem Is . . .

A poem can be enjoyful
A poem can make you down

A poem can be an epic
And quite often, the poem can be dull . . .

A poem is like the galaxy, with many words as worlds,
Dotted . . . around . . . the . . . paper, in a clever way to be heard.

A poem can rhyme from time to time
Like a bell which, when needed, chimes.

The poetry, poets and their many skills will never end
For it is a very long running trend.

Stories of myths and legends
Some, sometimes, with an unknown end.

Thomas Brown (14)
St Aidan's County High School, Carlisle

My Journey

M agical myths
Y esterday I started my journey.

J umping in the squashy mud
O n the boat to Africa,
U nwell, I am seasick.
R eally very jolly
N ever sad
E ating cream cakes, I'm very glad,
Y ippie! I'm on my way home.

Courtney Gray (12)
St Aidan's County High School, Carlisle

My Journey

C arlisle are in the final
A nd they'll be strong
R oad to Wembley
L DV finals is for football teams that aren't in the Premiership
I s the cup ours?
S top, he's offside!
L et's go home
E nd of game.

Jonny Burrow (13)
St Aidan's County High School, Carlisle

As I Was Walking

I was walking through a wood,
White turned to brown as we stomped in the mud.
With trees that were green.
Beautiful and colourful, was everything I seen.
Acorns were brown,
Leaves, crisp and golden, like a crown.
A house made of trees,
A place to sit and have some tea.
Some trees tall,
Some trees small.
Stumps to sit on,
As our walk was really long.
This is our journey
A journey I went on.

Laura Johnson
St Aidan's County High School, Carlisle

My Journey

Bobbing and swaying down the lanes,
Me and my family speeding away,
Beep! Beep! Beep!
As we go into Dover.
Beep! Beep! Beep!
As we soon get closer
To the great port of Dover.

Jade Ullyart (13)
St Aidan's County High School, Carlisle

Trinidad And Tobago

M y family and I left Trinidad and Tobago
Y awning my head off, feeling sad and bored

J umbled all my stuff together with ferment
O rganised all the suitcases together
U pset and lonely was the way I felt
R unning to the departure gate, making sure I was on time
N ervously went through the security gates
E stimating how much time we had to embark
'Y ou are free to go now,' said the Embassy Officer.

Samantha Joseph (14)
St Aidan's County High School, Carlisle

Child Life

As a child
I'd lots of fun,
loved a lot by Dad
and Mum, as I grew
to be older, more
responsibility was on
my shoulder to pass exams,
a job to get, the time is going
I enjoy it yet, I've a lot to do still
with my life, to be happy, secure,
and I may be a wife, in time to come,
When I am grown, to start a family of my
own, and when I'm older and in your shoes,
I'll pass on wisdom with my views.
One day I may be old and wise
and my life will have been
made with lows and highs.

Charlotte Jenkins (14)
St Aidan's County High School, Carlisle

Hallowe'en

Hallowe'en is here
And ghosts will appear

Witches of the west
Come greatly dressed

Knock, knock on my door
Candy please, a little bit more

So Hallowe'en is here
And ghosts will appear
Remember Hallowe'en is fun
It has only just begun.

Holly Salisbury (11)
St Ambrose Barlow RC High School, Swinton

My First Day

In the corridor
stood alone and feeling scared,
Year Eleven's messing around,
turn around,
My friends were there!

Walking to lesson in a bunch,
looking and feeling fine,
Until we noticed
we were lost
and it was half-nine!

'Go to lesson,'
teacher shouted.
Apologised sweetly
and threw in a smile.

Got home,
feeling glad,
about the day
I'd just had!

Shellie Skillen (11)
St Ambrose Barlow RC High School, Swinton

My First Day At High School!

Knees trembling, hands shaking
as my first day began,
lots of new faces
new people to meet.
Please help me find my seat.

The sound of the bell
break time begins,
pushing and shoving
everyone rushing.
Standing with my friends from primary school
hoping I don't look like such a fool.

The day ends at last
I'm on my way home,
the worries and fears have left me alone
I've made some new friends,
I've found my way round
the toast looks so tasty
I must remember my pound!

Savannah Louise Palmer (12)
St Ambrose Barlow RC High School, Swinton

First Day Of High School

I was really nervous about starting school,
Everyone told me silly rumours like
Getting your head flushed down the toilet!
I knew it wasn't going to happen.

When I arrived, it looked really big,
Everyone was standing around.
Brand new school shoes,
Brand new uniforms.

The teacher showed us to the hall,
Where we sat for assembly.
Mrs Murphy told us what was going to happen,
They read out lots of names,
Mine came and I was with my friends!

It came to the end of the day,
It had gone really fast!
I had met new friends who were
Really great!

Ellie McHugh (11)
St Ambrose Barlow RC High School, Swinton

My First Day

This is a story
about my first day at this school,
and all the reasons why
it didn't turn out so cool.

Lots of parents waiting outside my gate,
to see their little children
off on their first day.
So off we went on our first day
tried to get to school but we got
lost along the way!

So there we were in the main hall
and there we were sorted.
But I got split up from my best mate
and then I was gutted.

And there I was without a friend,
but I remembered it was not the end.
Then we had playtime,
and got soaked, wet through!

Then came the end of the day,
can't believe I made it, phew!
At least I can go home now,
hip hip hooray, woohoo!

Kieran McMullen (11)
St Ambrose Barlow RC High School, Swinton

My First Day!

You could get your head flushed down the loo,
My sister said it would happen to you.

I was very scared and nervous too,
I wanted to pretend I had the flu.

As I walked through the gate,
I was glad to know I wasn't late.

I saw my friends in the yard,
I was relieved, it didn't seem too hard.

I was scared that I would get lost,
I didn't know how much dinners cost.

I entered the classroom, it was okay,
Now I knew I would have a good day.

Jodie Loughrey (11)
St Ambrose Barlow RC High School, Swinton

My First Day . . .

First day blues,
Rubbing new shoes.
New blazer and tie,
Feeling uneasy and shy.

Timetable to remember,
It'll take me 'til December!
Turn left to room two,
But where is the loo . . . ?

Late and lost in the science block,
Keeping a close eye on the clock.
Learning by the teacher's way,
It's a very busy day!

At dinner time we stop to eat,
Finally I'm finding my feet.
At home time, my nerves drift away,
It hasn't been a bad first day.

Amy Concannon (11)
St Ambrose Barlow RC High School, Swinton

My First Day

Butterflies in my stomach
High school's on its way
I'm wondering what it's like
It's my very first day

I've heard so many stories
I'll guess I'll just have to wait and see
Just exactly what the day
Will hold in store for me.

As I wait nervously at the gate
For a friendly face to see
My thoughts turn back to primary school
Where everybody knew me.

People I don't know
Come to see
If I am okay
And talk to me.

I have to meet my teachers
They all seem really cool
There's so many to get to know,
In this really big school.

My day is nearly over
I've made so many friends
I can't wait until tomorrow
I hope it never ends.

High school isn't so scary
Just you wait and see
It all makes up the best
Memories for me.

Jade Carroll (11)
St Ambrose Barlow RC High School, Swinton

My First Day At School

My first day at school
would I be cool?
Would I fit in,
or end up a fool?

Would I get lost,
like a rat in a maze?
Or bullied and tortured
throughout my school days?

Would I end up starving?
Would schoolwork be hard?
Would I suffer and toil
for no real reward?

I pondered and puzzled,
exercising my brain.
I thought and I thought
nearly going insane.

But I ended up liking
my first day at school,
Making mates, having fun;
it was all really cool!

Niall Whitehead (12)
St Ambrose Barlow RC High School, Swinton

My First Day At Senior School

At first I thought that senior school
Would be really cool.
But I'd heard some scary tales
That sent me off the rails.
So I just thought, *when I walk through those gates,*
I'll be there with my mates.

My best friend was put in 7C,
I was in 7W but I was relieved to see
That two of my mates were also there
With their new uniform and smartly cut hair.
So the three of us went to our first lesson - art,
And we walked down the corridor
looking really smart.

Then at break, I met my friend,
Who'd been waiting for his lesson to end.
So he could talk till break's end,
about not being with a friend.
Then we chose a meeting place,
which we could call our home base.

Daniel Jenkinson (11)
St Ambrose Barlow RC High School, Swinton

My First Day At High School

Getting your head flushed down the toilet,
Is this really true?
The rumours are starting to get to me,
did they get to you?

The nerves were attacking me,
I felt so small,
everywhere was big and everyone
so tall!

I felt like running, running away,
running back to primary school,
where I got a say!

Everyone was older,
I felt trapped inside.
I needed to hold my head high
and walk with pride.

I was unable to do this,
I felt so shy,
I wanted to go home
and break down and cry.

I walked through the gate,
a smile headed my way,
after all the worrying,
it seemed okay.

People ran up to me
asked me my name,
I said it proudly,
I said it with no shame.

I like my school,
it's not that bad,
after all that
I shouldn't have been sad.

Alex Pantegi (11)
St Ambrose Barlow RC High School, Swinton

My First Day At St Ambrose Barlow

I need a book
A bigger bag
I need a map
And a name tag.

I need some pencils
I need a ruler,
Maybe some earrings,
To make me look cooler.

I'm in a rush,
It's a quarter to nine,
Oh, just relax,
It's going to be fine!

I've just arrived,
I'm in a form,
The pressure's on,
Wow! It's warm.

I've met my teachers,
I've got my books.
I've met new people
And got some funny looks!

Everybody's so big,
I feel as small as a gnome,
Oh yes, there's a bell
It's time for us all to go home!

Gemma Robinson (12)
St Ambrose Barlow RC High School, Swinton

My First Day

It was my first day at school today,
The butterflies in my tummy wouldn't go away.

I heard bad rumours off all my friends,
I wanted to be ill, I thought I might pretend!

People said I'd get my head flushed down the loo,
But I wasn't sure if that was actually true.

My mum dropped me off down the street,
I couldn't see my friend who I was supposed to meet.

I wasn't so sure where to go,
Then I saw Jodie who also didn't know.

What was I supposed to do? I hadn't a clue,
Then we saw the playground full of people we knew!

I saw year 8s and 9s and year 10, all acting so cool,
Walking past them, I felt such a fool.

We went into the hall and all sat down,
We were told our forms, I couldn't frown.

Once I got into the classroom, I was okay,
And in the end I had a great day!

Jessica Kehoe (11)
St Ambrose Barlow RC High School, Swinton

Getting Ready For High School!

Getting ready for high school,
Made me think about,
The things that people have told me
Like how the teachers shout!

Walking down with all my friends,
Really, really nervous.
Bump into some Year Eleven lad,
Who thinks I've done it on purpose!

Meet my form,
Only some people I know,
So when it came to talking,
I just went with the flow!

Find out about all my new teachers,
Turns out my luck has begun!
For lunch, I have a pizza
With cheese on it and ham!

Then we have more lessons,
And finally double PE.
Nobody has their kit
So we play games and partner into 3!

Finally the day is over,
We all are really tired!
When we get home and tell our younger siblings
They are really inspired!

Ilaria Arnetoli (11)
St Ambrose Barlow RC High School, Swinton

My First Day

The holidays were over,
We were back to school soon.
I'd bought all my equipment,
Ready for a new classroom.

I'd heard horrific rumours,
Involving people's heads and the loo,
We were warned of evil teachers,
I prayed these things weren't true.

I tried on my new uniform,
I wasn't keen at first,
But slowly over time
I realised it wasn't the worst.

I left on my first morning,
Feeling pessimistic and scared.
I was soon going to find out
How primary school compared.

When I got there, the school was
Much bigger than I remembered.
When I first came and visited,
Early last September.

I was quickly assigned to my form tutor,
Who I think I'm going to like,
And by that time, to my surprise,
I began to feel alright.

There was a similar story to that,
All throughout the day,
I had a great time in all my classes,
I honestly have to say.

Although it's not been long
I have enjoyed my time at school.
Considering I thought it'd be quite rubbish
It really has been cool.

Daniel McNorton (11)
St Ambrose Barlow RC High School, Swinton

First Day At High School

The holidays are over; it's high school tomorrow,
I don't think I want to go!
Getting my head flushed down the loo
doesn't sound like much fun,
why didn't I go to a convent school
and become a nun.

I remember my first day,
all I did was pray, that I wasn't
the odd one out.
That my teachers didn't scream and shout.

That I'd fit right in and look the part,
I knew I did because I was smart,
in my uniform I stood and knew that I would
make my parents feel good in my heart.

Meghan Reece (11)
St Ambrose Barlow RC High School, Swinton

First Day At School

I turned up for school
Happy as can be,
I looked around
To see who I could see.

As we got into form,
I wanted all my friends.
I found out I had none of them
But made new ones.

As I talked to my new people,
I got to know them and see what they were like,
But then the day was over and I got to go home.

Thomas Tuohy (11)
St Ambrose Barlow RC High School, Swinton

First Day Of School

I got out of the car and stared at the gate
waiting for my old best mate,
The school looked gigantic with lots of kids
throwing liquid-filled bottles without lids.

The bottles flew over our heads just like missiles
the teachers came out blowing they're whistles,
We walked into the hall in a straight line
we found out our forms, and my friend was in mine.

We went into our forms and found out our classes
but we had to go down the stairs where everyone dashes,
There was pushing, shoving and running followed by
a long long queue.
We soon realised you had to get there early
unless it'd happen to you.

The end of the day was nearly there,
we could leave the school without a care.
Go home and relax watching TV
my first day at Ambrose Barlow High School RC.

Rachael Stanton (11)
St Ambrose Barlow RC High School, Swinton

My First Day At School

My first day at school,
Well what can I say?
We went to lessons
And had time to play!

My first day at school,
Well what would I do?
Would it be the same
Or would it be new?

My first day at school,
Well what would I be?
Would I be cool?
Would they like me?

My first day at school,
Well how would I know
What to do
Or where to go?

My first day at school
Well what can I say?
I made new friends
And had a great day!

Leah Shannon (11)
St Ambrose Barlow RC High School, Swinton

On Your First Day Of High School!

Walking round the corridors
Getting lost,
Where are all my classes
And how much does lunch cost?

Meeting new people,
Making new friends,
Late for my lesson
Going round the bend!

Forgetting my homework, forgetting my pen
Teachers say the same thing again and again . . .
Code of conduct! Red writing! Detention!

So to all you Year 7s starting high school
Listen and pay attention!
Don't be a fool
Be prepared for high school!

Chelsea McIntosh (11)
St Ambrose Barlow RC High School, Swinton

My First Day

My first day at a new child prison

I really didn't want to get
My head flushed down the loo,
On the morning of my first day
I wanted to fake the flu.

Like nervous little lambs,
We were so small.
Compared to the Year 11s
They towered above us all.

But now we're a bit more at home,
In our high school, we wouldn't
Dare to moan!

Shannon Sackfield (12)
St Ambrose Barlow RC High School, Swinton

Winter Poem

W inter is the best time of the year,
  I t's the time when everyone gives a Christmas cheer
N ice white snow falling from above
T ime for toasty woolly gloves
E veryone enjoys the soft white snow,
R olling snowballs to throw at people you know!

Jordan Stephens (11)
St Ambrose Barlow RC High School, Swinton

Autumn

I spin around in the golden sunbeam
ready for it to pick me up and take me away.

I tremble on the amber leaves and throw
them up into the sapphire sky.

I lie on the soft-dewed grass watching the
rainbow birds whizz past.

I love it when you wake up and look out of the window
and see the golden ball in the sky.

Some day I wish a bird would just take me
up into that crystal-blue sky.

Eve Leary (11)
St Ambrose Barlow RC High School, Swinton

My Cat

Dave Cooper is our cat
He likes to sleep
And eats lots of food
Making him big and fat.

Most of the time he lives in the house
But sometimes he goes into the garden
To eat spiders and flies
And look for a mouse.

He has ginger fur and white paws
Sometimes he hides under the sofa
For peace and quiet
But when we walk past, he sticks out his claws.

He is quite cute and makes us laugh,
And he likes being brushed.
But one thing he doesn't like
Is having a bath!

Emily Cooper (11)
St Ambrose Barlow RC High School, Swinton

The Weather Report

We wake in the morning to bright sunlight,
It beats down upon us with all its might.
The plants and grass absorb its food
And it helps us to improve our mood.
As the day moves on, the clouds appear,
They smother the sun which is our fear
All is good as the birds sing their song,
Everything that was right, now so wrong.
The clouds blacken as the rain begins to fall,
Showing no mercy to one and all.
What began as a pleasant cool breeze,
Had whipped up its prisoners, it began to seize.

We have had all the seasons in 24 hours,
From sun to cloud and plenty of showers.
And now I'm at the end of my tether,
But I suppose that's down to the Manchester weather.

Sean Brady (11)
St Ambrose Barlow RC High School, Swinton

The Race

Waiting, stood still, feeling sick,
Listen for one sound.
You stand on the block, looking straight ahead,
Searching for a way out
Too late, the horn goes.

You dive into the water,
Your mind goes blank.
All you can hear is your heart beating.
More scared now, coming up to the first turn,
A deep breath and you're over.

You see others beside you,
You swim faster.
Here comes your next turn,
Another deep breath.
Under the water you go.

Faster and faster,
Getting very tired.
But you want to win,
Gritting your teeth.
As you swim faster.

The last turn is straight ahead,
You take a deep breath.
Then upside down as you go,
Other people are catching up,
But you want to win.

You hit the wall
And you have won.
Your team are shouting
You go up and collect your trophy.
You start laughing and say
Why was I so scared of that?

Lucy Cavannagh (11)
St Ambrose Barlow RC High School, Swinton

Holidays In The Sun

Walking on the sand
Crunching on your feet,
The shimmering shores,
A luscious treat.

The golden glowing sun,
Gleaming in the sky.
Shining down on the blue horizon,
A shame to say goodbye.

Exotic as can be
A dazzling sight to see.

Jessica Chappell (11)
St Ambrose Barlow RC High School, Swinton

My Holiday In Mexico

A place for seeking adventure,
The luscious jungle landscapes of the Sierra Nevada.
Stunning sandy beaches to play on,
And fabulous sunsets to watch in the evening.

A place to relax, rest or explore,
Sweltering heat and tropical storms.
Swim this way, walk that way,
There'll always be more.

Cosmopolitan atmosphere, with Mexican charm,
Vibrant colours and rainbow fabrics.
Red-tiled roofs and white-washed walls,
The exquisite cathedral of Guadeloupe.

Migratory whales return to the Pacific Coast to breed,
On palm-filled shores loggerhead turtles lay their eggs.
Fun-filled days with friendly dolphins,
Exotic iguanas wandering walkways.

Amy Burns (11)
St Ambrose Barlow RC High School, Swinton

My Past To My Future!

I stood at St Charles
to bid them goodbye,
Six weeks later I was
standing in the hall of my Senior High,
I met new friends, old and new
this future is kind of hard
at getting used to!

The hall is very long,
the classrooms are slightly big,
Oh how I miss the days of
being in Year 6.

Four years time, I'll sit my exams
and plan my career,
Before I realise, my future
is here!

I've found my chosen profession
I can be a make-up artist
which is my chosen career.
And that was the past to the
future for me!

Kayleigh Anna Hawkins (11)
St Ambrose Barlow RC High School, Swinton

Catch Of The Day

Just before dawn
The boat slipped away,
As the gulls took flight
They followed it on its way.
Far out at sea
The boat bobbled about.
The men cast their net
Deep into the sea,
As the gulls dived about
They hauled up the net
To see what they had got
The captain gasped with delight
And picked up a big fish.
Down from the sky there
Was a mighty swish.
The gull took the fish.

Lewis McCaffery (11)
St Ambrose Barlow RC High School, Swinton

School Time!

S chool is fun, school is great
C hildren running through the gate
H omework quickly piles up
O h can I have your red book?
O ut come children, wild and mad
L ike yesterday I am first in line,
    Mmm! ice cream is fine!

Amy Farlow (12)
St Ambrose Barlow RC High School, Swinton

My Poem

Year 7 is the best
better than the rest,

Year 8 is late,
still outside the gate.

Year 9 is on time,
ready to get in line.

Year 10 are looking for Ben,
he's in trouble again.

Year 11, it's not Heaven,
looking after year seven.

Harry Heardman (11)
St Ambrose Barlow RC High School, Swinton

Hallowe'en

Green cats' eyes
following you!
A ghost curse
stuck on you!
Bones being discovered,
old and new!
Witches stirring a horrible
great big stew
all for me and you!

Mark Jennings (11)
St Ambrose Barlow RC High School, Swinton

Best Friends

B oth of us, we are so close,
E njoying each other's funny jokes.
S pecial you are to me,
T alking very happily.

F riends around you, they will say, 'Are you coming out to play?'
R ebecca's birthday is in May but . . .
I sabel's birthday is much further away.
E very day you should laugh,
N ever fall out because that's daft.
D ogs are our favourite pet.
S o glad that we met!

Bethany Wakefield (11)
St Ambrose Barlow RC High School, Swinton

My First Day At Secondary School

Is it cos I'm worried?
Is it cos I'm scared?
Are the rumours true?
Is my head going down the loo?

Why do I want to run?
Why do I want to hide?
'You'll love it!' they all say,
I don't feel so sure inside.

The morning's finally come,
I'm up before the sun!
My friends are going to call,
They're downstairs in the hall.

I'm walking in the yard,
Hey, this is not too hard!
There are lots of brand new faces
Trying to find their places.

During my first day I found
High school was OK for now.
The lessons were not long,
Hey, this sounds like a song!

Jessica Houten (11)
St Ambrose Barlow RC High School, Swinton

High School Poem

H is for a huge step in life.

I is for all the interesting new things I will learn.

G is for all the good new friends I'll make.

H is for happy, that is what I am now in high school.

S is for sad that I have left primary.

C is for all the new cool teachers.

H is for all the homework I'll get.

O is for outings and lots to see.

O is for an opportunity of a lifetime.

L is for learning all new things.

Jake Eckersley (11)
St Ambrose Barlow RC High School, Swinton

Limeramble

There was a witch called Constance
Who loved to talk loads of nonsense
She lived in a swamp with a tomcat called Tom
No one knew where he was from.
One day he felt very funny and felt a rumbling in his tummy,
So he decided to drink some milk.
He mixed it with slime and a dash of wine
And of course he was drunk.
He dyed his fur so he looked like a punk
And then he turned into a big, fat, punky skunk.

Niall McCormick
St Benedict's RC School, Whitehaven

Looking Through A Window

Their eyes upon me
Gazing through me
Never at me
Always staring.

Life continues on as I hang here
suspended on an iron frame
Opening and closing
To keep me entertained.

Rivers, lakes and trees pass me by
As I sit and wait in my cosy corner of beauty
I shall always be here for ever and ever
But I did not see the great brick circling towards me
Shattering me forever.

I now have a thousand lives, not just one.

Tom Kelly
St Benedict's RC School, Whitehaven

Alone I Sit

Alone I sit.
Well, I'm not actually.
I want
To be alone
But I'm not.

I wish everything would work out right.
Very naïve.
Expectations of success
Creep in from every direction,
Until I am submerged.

Alone I sit.
Well, I'm not actually.
I want
To be alone
But I'm not.

I wish for someone to hold me.
Very naïve
Expectations of warmth and love and happiness,
But that would be a fairy tale, or a dream,
And we all know that dreams and wishes don't come true.

Alone I sit.
Well, I am actually.

Grace Littler (14)
St Michael's RC Secondary School, Billingham

You

You are a Belgium chocolate,
With your best part inside,
Deliciously handsome, yet mild.
You are a raindrop on a rose,
Streaking its velvety skin.
You are the tear,
Streaking my skin right now.
You are a ray of sunlight,
Through the closed window,
Reminding me of the promise of new life.
You have the mouth,
That is a forgiving smile,
Forgetting what has been done.
And your eyes
Are honest,
As honest as a white, white cloud.
You are the scarf
Keeping me warm,
Not letting me go
Despite what I have done.
You are a glove
And I am your partner,
Your match, your pair.
You are the first, the only star that shines at night,
Twinkling in the midst of the darkness.
My beacon, my hope, my love.
A pity, it is,
For you are all of these things.
And me?
I am nothing - at least that's what you see.

Felicity Jayne Reeves (15)
St Michael's RC Secondary School, Billingham

The Man In Black

A man in black is strolling down the road
He won a bravery award last week,
'You're going to ace your physics course,' his college teacher told
He takes a left turn down an alley, heading for home
Next morning his bag would be discovered with 'brave?'
written on in bold

He walks past a gang in white-hooded cloaks
They see him, and with a nod they follow
Their intentions are hostile, they want to see this boy broke
He turns round as he hears footsteps
He realises his fate, and knows this isn't a hoax

The gang realise he knows, and go in for the kill
Let's see how brave you are now
They set upon him and on the pavement does his blood spill
After the beating they deface his bag and throw it away
Before they make off down the hill.

The man lies there in the pouring rain
He is not clear on what just happened
What did I do to deserve this pain?
What was the motivation of this attack?
Whatever it was, I now lie here in shame.

Joe Tyrer (14)
St Michael's RC Secondary School, Billingham

Dreams

I lay awake last night in bed, I saw a face before my head
The face was of a friend but he was long dead
His eyes began burning in fire
His screams rose higher and higher
A knife rose up and then plunged down
His face, evil, now was a staring frown
The knife it passed through the sheets
A hand rose up as if to greet
My soul to Heaven or to Hell
I was woken by the noise of a ringing bell
Then I looked and turned bright green
It had not been just a dream.

David Gopsill (14)
Trinity School, Carlisle

My Best Friend

I have no best friend
No best friend for me
But there are some
Friends I do have
So this poem's not all about me
My first friend is a fast guy
He can outrun anyone I know
My second friend is a smart guy
A brainiac if you please
But instead of using his book smarts
He helps me when I'm down in heart
My next friend's a regular friend
Who does the same things as me
Then there's my newest friend
We laugh, we jump and play around
Always not making a sound
So don't feel sorry for me
I'm the luckiest kid in the world
I don't have a best friend
I have four.

Alexander Murray (11)
Trinity School, Carlisle

Cat

The cat came and went through the flap and outside.
It slid onto the box, the brown, creased box,
and then it vanished, as if it was never there.

As it came, it slid and slipped
on the slippery surface
and then . . .

Heather Medley (11)
Trinity School, Carlisle

Crush

There's this girl I like, you know,
Her name's a mystery.
Every day her cheeks glow,
She really hates history.

Her hair is black and straight,
Like a waterfall of blackened hair.
And for the bus she's never late,
She always walks with care.

I really like this girl you know,
She smiles at me through the windowpane.
If she likes me she'll never show,
Because if she doesn't like me I will be filled with pain.

Ben Kerfoot (12)
Trinity School, Carlisle

The Cold

The cold . . .
The cold that wakes me up every morning.
The cold that puts me to bed.
The howling winds which over time seems to be talking.
But is this the paranoia of a fun-starved mind?
Working . . .
Working, starting to become second
Nature, same old routine.
I wish . . .
I wish that the life I used to have
The life which I had intended to have
Was mine once more, back in my country
Iceland . . .
Iceland where the snow covers the fields
And where my family are.
But I have been driven out to London
Where my living nightmare lives!

Martin Shaw (14)
Trinity School, Carlisle

I Miss Cumbria

Living in Australia is nice but I do so miss Cumbria.
I miss the deep green and yellow mountains
Capped with white dots of the sheep grazing peacefully.
The pale blue lakes on which ducks swim and men fish.
Also I miss the gentle swoosh of the river washing over the pebbles.
It was only this morning I thought I heard a cow mooing.
Alas though it was only a motorbike going by.
Dusty Australia is not like Cumbria at all really.
No green hills or pale lakes.
Just miles of barren desert which the warm south wind
Swirls around blowing the cactus trees.
As I lie my head back to rest I can hear Cumbria calling.
Soon I shall be back in the rolling countryside of beautiful Cumbria.

Mark Scott (14)
Trinity School, Carlisle

The Peace Garden

Mint-green grass spreads as far as the eye can see,
The bulky hedge a spiky, curled up hedgehog
Hiding from its predators.
The golden light rays shining down
Revealing the dark and evil side to every living thing.
On the end of every stroke and blade
A silver starlight shines.
Over-towering silhouettes look down upon the Earth,
The Earth so good, the Earth so great,
The Earth that we destroy.
Why can't this beauty live on for ever
For generations to enjoy?

Amy Walker (11)
Trinity School, Carlisle

Zany!

Zany and crazy, it hangs on a wall,
Watching the world go by.
I can feel it drawing me in,
Enticing me with its dark but bright colours.
It pulls and pulls, like an excited dog on a lead.
It's like I'm falling, falling into its moody depths.

It reflects the way I feel, the way I live my life.
It reflects my personality, the way I smile,
The way I laugh, the way I enjoy myself.
It is totally and utterly me.

Hannah Cook (11)
Trinity School, Carlisle

Colours Of Love

Oranges and reds, flames of happiness,
Light of love is the sun.
The green bush is bright as an emerald.
Purples and whites creep up the emeralds
Like a lurking cat.
Shadowed horse like a cloud
Will hang over them forever.
But happiness glides with the delicate blues
Which dance around the skies.
Heartbreak is over for the mourning march.

Colours of love danced in a swirl.
Fireworks shot out and made a smile
Swish, swish.
His life should now be perfect
As long as it stays as it is.

Alice Hodgson (11)
Trinity School, Carlisle

War

The thick slurred mud, grasping at our ankles,
Like the wretched men who went before us.
My neighbours' sweat, stale and stagnant, poisoning the air.
Marching, always marching, one foot after another,
Trudging onwards till blood pours.
The explosions, a continual drone, drilling into my mind,
Killing the sweet dream of home.
I turn my battered head towards the blood-red sun,
The sky filled with predatory birds.

I beat the tears from my eyes,
I will not cave, I will not cry.
I'll make you proud,
I'll make you smile,
I'll make our children remember my name.

My brother left last week, just another prisoner of death.
I saw the realisation dawn in his eyes.
I saw the pain tear at his lungs.
I saw his blood bubble from his mouth.
I saw his eyes dim, and see no more.
I heard his screams rent the night.
I heard his body being removed.
I heard our friends weep.
I heard his death bell toll, too quickly drowned out.
I saw his few treasures being collected,
The photos he looked at, the letters he read.

I beat the tears from my eyes
I will not cave, I will not cry.
I'll make you proud,
I'll make you smile,
I'll make our children remember my name.

Sarah-Louise Hetherington (15)
Trinity School, Carlisle

Old

I'm old now
In my wooden chair
My wrinkled old skin
My shiny silver hair.
I looked through the glass window
Into the calm day.
The sky changes colour
From golden blue to grey
To black.
I'm there in these dark
Wastelands.
Back in my house
I remember it like it was yesterday
The worst day of my life.
It smashed
Crashed and pummelled
My house.
Flash, I'm back.

Moses Hill (15)
Witherslack Hall School, Grange-over-Sands

Criminals

Thundering and lightning.
It's dark and death-like.
Like a mixed-up boy in an abused life
Dark, very dark.
Angry like a raging bull in a bullfight.
Like a Ferrari with a killer behind the wheel.
Its partner in crime is warm and cosy
Like a young child awakening to Christmas Day.
Like newborn puppies cuddling up to their mother.
But he also has a devilish side with him
Murdering hundreds of people every day
Through cancer and dehydration.
But no prison can hold something so big
But if there was, would it help?

Craig Neal (15)
Witherslack Hall School, Grange-over-Sands

Anti-Bullying

Bullying is bad
Bullying makes people sad
Bullying makes people hide
Which means they lose their pride
Bullying is really wrong
It can affect you all day long
Bullies only do it because they think they're big and strong.

But I know that bullying is really wrong
Being bullied puts you down
You no longer want to be around
Bullying sometimes makes you cry
And sometimes want to wish to die.

Don't keep your fear inside
Tell someone and retrieve your pride
Beat the bullies at their game
Make them the ones who feel the shame.

Jamie Crowie (14)
Witherslack Hall School, Grange-over-Sands

Bullying Poem

You get it for being English
You get it for being slack
You get it for being sick
You get it for turning your back.

You get it for being thin
You get it for being fat
You get it for your religion
You get it for this and that.

The bullies who do these things aren't perfect.
The bullies are really cowards
The bullies think they are really tough.
But really they are not.
But really they are not.

Jordan Ogden (14)
Witherslack Hall School, Grange-over-Sands

Bullying

B ullying is wrong
U se people to talk to.
L ike to have friends
L ive life full, not getting bullied
Y ou don't like it, so don't do it to others
I would speak to people
N o one likes it
G et a life not being bullied.

Chris Richardson (14)
Witherslack Hall School, Grange-over-Sands

Bullying

They only pick on him
Because he doesn't fight back
They call him loads of names
Because he doesn't fight back
They wind him up
Because he doesn't fight back.

I don't fight back
Because I get scared
I don't fight back
Because they beat me up
I don't fight back
Because I can't be bothered

Two different ways
Of dealing with bullies.

Aidon Pinder (13)
Witherslack Hall School, Grange-over-Sands

Little Jimmy

It was little Jimmy's
First day at school
Walked into the classroom
And got laughed at like a fool.

Got bullied for his teeth
Got bullied for his hair
Got bullied for everything
And it really wasn't fair.

He told staff
They didn't care

He told parents
They didn't care

Jimmy just thought
He would rather have died
So that's what he did
Committed suicide.

Alexander Stubbs (14)
Witherslack Hall School, Grange-over-Sands

Bullies

I was bullied at school
Everybody called me a fool
Everybody offered me a duel

I didn't dare go to school because I was being bullied
I was hurried, hurried, hurried
I was always scared
I hate being bullied!

I started to be bad
I felt sad
There's more to life than this
But no one is listening to me
Nobody cares about me
I hate being bullied!

James Leggatt (14)
Witherslack Hall School, Grange-over-Sands

Bullying

Walking into the trap
Mum's gone home
I know I will get teased and can't get home

Inside I'm saying, 'Help me!'
Outside I look like a freak

I am too scared to ask for help
Scared people will take the mick out of me
Sitting there all alone
No one to help me.

Patrick Burton (14)
Witherslack Hall School, Grange-over-Sands

No Diving - Haiku

'No diving' states the
sign, all rules defied, movement
caught frozen in time.

David Bradley (17)
Xaverian College, Manchester

Bus Route Journeys

Walked in the rain for a while to
The ending note of a Danse macabre.
Concrete jungle and back-beat kids.
Fascination with a shade of red.
The trailing of fingers along garden walls
To an off-beat, down the pavement.

Bleeding, bitter eyes watched, hurrying figures in coats,
Place to place, a business loop.
From a place within a place,
Beyond the flesh within a dream. See
Hair the colour of a carnation, from a bottle.
A plastic bag and an awful limp.
Jaunty twitches to a deadpan ringtone, a corporate catalogue.

Without, within, an alien conscience.
An elevation below their feet.
A glass roof. Silence, sound permeates.

Emma Tillyer (17)
Xaverian College, Manchester

Revolution - Haikus

'Fight the power!' cries
An empowered woman from
The great gathering.

Enthused, spirited,
Advocates of China's might:
Defiant, ready.

Jennifer Lear (16)
Xaverian College, Manchester

Fingers That Beat Upon A Drum

Away he flees away from me, a committed marriage is not what I see.
His cool superior, his frightful stare has caused me to turn
and hide in fear.
Oblivious anger his mind has learned which through all failure
has not turned.
I wish to fly, to fly away, to soar the sky and be astray.

Deceit, torture, anger and lies.
Now you wonder why I cry.

Knock, knock on Heaven's door, I live below on Hell's floor.
Each touch, each kiss, each memorable embrace, scorches me
to a confided hate.
An animal, a cowardly beast, a savage in the moment of heat.
A hateful hit, a raging shout can only bring me to more doubt.
Imprisoned I am his slave to keep, to beat, to kick, to scream,
Life is nothing more than of what it seems.

Deceit, torture, anger and lies.
Now you wonder why I cry.

How this one man has shattered me so, I nothing more than his
upcoming hoe.
A hoe I am that's what he says when he takes me down and
lays his head.
Cold and stiff he takes me there, forcing his hands throughout my hair.
He sickens me throughout all height as he groans his pleasure
with his worldly might.
Bang, bang, bang as his footsteps near, and cower I in fear.

Deceit, torture, anger and lies.
Now you wonder why I cry.

A devoted companion he once was, but now I realise that's at loss.
His many kisses, his sweet devotion, but all gone to a hateful emotion.
Away he goes, away from me, further apart shall we be.
My life is his, there is no more bliss, it is at an end
So shall we meet again.

Dominique Ambrose (16)
Xaverian College, Manchester

Opaque

It's as if you do not see me
I'm invisible, transparent
Just a ghost, or a shadow
Unseen, unheard of, undetectable
Like a glimpse of hope
That fizzles away
Like a shooting star
Gone before you had a chance to capture its image
A challenge you cannot meet
Nor visualise, is somewhat like me
Unable to hear, see or touch
Too small to see with your blurred eyes
And yet, your eyes are not obscured
Still, you fail to set eyes on me
As if I do not exist
As if I am an angel from Heaven
No one can say that I am real
And still, I am valid
I am true and genuine
So what if I am unknown?
Will the world still keep turning when I am gone?
Yes, the world shall still spin
As no one will notice I have left this life
Maybe one day, someone will perceive my absence
And they shall wonder for evermore what happened to me
My apparent translucent existence
Makes me seem disappeared
And yet I am actually opaque
The girl that sits in the corner
Nose in a book
Hands scribbling the thoughts of her psyche
And you do not succeed to take notice of me
It's true, I am quiet and hushed
Like a butterfly, fluttering her wings

But I am still here
In this life
One day you will notice me
When I am being thunderous
And I have made my mark on this planet
You shall see me
In all my glory
And then you will remember me
The girl who was opaque, translucent, transparent.

Kirsty Nicol-Brown (16)
Xaverian College, Manchester

Bitter-Sweet

Stone-cold eyes
That mask the pain inside
The blood-red lips that taunt you
The blood-red smile that daunts you
The muttered curses that haunt you
Behind the sickly sweet compliments
The all-consuming fire
Of anger and desire
That lashes out with smouldering tongue
And whiplash wit
The affectionate kiss of friendship
That bites down on bloody lips
Spits poison and whispers:
'I love you.'

Maili McQuaid (17)
Xaverian College, Manchester

Be My Rock

You could be my rock:
be my shelter
be my temple

you could be my pillar:
shelter me from the rain
from the pain

you could be so much in my life
so much that you could gain

you could be the star in my night
the apple of my eye
the glint in my soul
my reason to live

so much potential
so many prospects

but no, I'm far too strong
and your weakness is far too great

to me you are my addiction
yet you are my aid

I want you to be my rock
but it will never
be that way.

Koreen Trumpet (16)
Xaverian College, Manchester

Young Writers Information

We hope you have enjoyed reading this book - and that you will continue to enjoy it in the coming years.

If you like reading and writing poetry drop us a line, or give us a call, and we'll send you a free information pack.

Alternatively if you would like to order further copies of this book or any of our other titles, then please give us a call or log onto our website at www.youngwriters.co.uk

**Young Writers Information
Remus House
Coltsfoot Drive
Peterborough
PE2 9JX**

(01733) 890066